I0463692

TALES *of a* TRIAL ATTORNEY

Twists and Turns of Litigation

SANFORD GOFFSTEIN

Copyright © 2016 Sanford Goffstein.

All rights reserved. No part of this book may be reproduced, stored, or
transmitted by any means—whether auditory, graphic, mechanical, or
electronic—without written permission of both publisher and author, except
in the case of brief excerpts used in critical articles and reviews. Unauthorized
reproduction of any part of this work is illegal and is punishable by law.

ISBN: 978-1-4834-5900-4 (sc)
ISBN: 978-1-4834-5899-1 (e)

Because of the dynamic nature of the Internet, any web addresses or links contained in
this book may have changed since publication and may no longer be valid. The views
expressed in this work are solely those of the author and do not necessarily reflect the
views of the publisher, and the publisher hereby disclaims any responsibility for them.

Any people depicted in stock imagery provided by Thinkstock are models,
and such images are being used for illustrative purposes only.
Certain stock imagery © Thinkstock.

Lulu Publishing Services rev. date: 10/06/2016

DEDICATION

I dedicate my first book to my best friend and wife, Phyllis. I look forward to each day we spend together. She has supported me in my work and in writing this book. I enjoy seeing her beautiful smile each and every day.

ACKNOWLEDGMENT

I want to thank my editor, Doris Gordon Liberman, for her direction and support in making sure my stories were completed. She was the first person to tell me that the stories I wrote were enjoyable and would be of interest to the general reading public in addition to those readers in the legal field.

I thank my partners, Don Sherman, Sanford Pomerantz, Jerry Kraus, and Lori Koch, each of whom played an important role in many of the cases in my law practice, but also the cases that are in this book. I have been fortunate to have their assistance for over 40 years with Don and Jerry, and 20 years for Sandy and Lori.

I am grateful to my friend, Professor Peter A. Joy, who is an outstanding professor of law at Washington University, St. Louis, for the positive comments he made about my book, as well as his comments about me as an adjunct professor for the Trial Practice and Procedure course.

I wish to thank Don Schlapprizzi, an outstanding trial attorney, for taking the time to read my manuscript and for his comments. Don is a well known trial attorney and member of the American College of Trial Lawyers. I have had the experience of sitting across the counsel table from Don as opposing counsel on several occasions.

I also want to express my gratitude to the professional photographer, Mark Katzman, for taking the time from his very busy schedule to provide a photograph for the cover of my book.

PREFACE

Sanford Goffstein has been a trial attorney for over 50 years. Most of his legal career has been defending professionals such as lawyers, doctors, accountants, insurance brokers, automobile dealers, among others. He has tried cases throughout the United States.

He graduated law school from Washington University in St. Louis in 1960 and immediately started his own law firm. In October 1961, just a little more than a year after starting his law firm, he was activated into the Air Force, as his Air National Guard unit was called to active duty as a result of the Berlin Wall being constructed. He had to close his law firm while on active duty and started again after serving one year in the service.

Sanford has served as an adjunct professor at Washington University, teaching trial practice and providing students his knowledge and personal experience in the trial of civil cases.

This is the first book written by the author. He has chosen stories that may bear some resemblance to actual cases he has handled, but for the most part, the names of the people are fictitious.

The author has attempted to show with these stories how interesting and enjoyable the life of a trial attorney can be. The author is continuing to try civil cases at 80 years of age and still enjoys the action in the courtroom.

FOREWORD

Washington University in St. Louis School of Law has been very fortunate to count Sanford "Sandy" Goffstein not only as an eminent alumnus, but as an outstanding Adjunct Professor in the Trial Practice & Procedure course. Sandy brings his considerable experience and knowledge as a trial lawyer who has litigated cases in scores of state and federal courts into the classroom as he instructs and counsels our law students not only on how to be an effective, ethical trial lawyer, but on how to find satisfaction, happiness, and success in the practice of law. Hundreds of Wash U. graduates and current students have personally benefitted from Sandy's instruction in the art of advocacy, and he has helped them learn that thorough preparation and carefully analyzing the law and facts lead to creative solutions to client problems both in and outside the courtroom. The cases he has chosen for this book provide insight not only into the enthusiasm, skill, and experience that he brings to each client's case, but his effectiveness as a both a trial lawyer and a great teacher.

July 19, 2016   Peter A. Joy
                       Henry Hitchcock Professor of Law
                       Washington University in St. Louis School of Law

CONTENTS

Chapter I   Protected Pension.. 1

Chapter II   Married in Death.. 47

Chapter III   The Defective Tractor................................ 57

Chapter IV   Fatal Reunion 80

Chapter V   Is Suicide Insurable?................................... 90

Chapter VI   The Phantom Vehicle.............................. 98

Chapter VII   Kiss in the Night 113

Chapter VIII   Last Clear Chance 118

CHAPTER I

PROTECTED PENSION

As an attorney looking to develop clients and build a successful legal career, your most important partner is your spouse. If you are fortunate enough to have one who is active, with a good personality, likeable, and makes friends easily, this could provide you with additional clients. My wife was an excellent partner not only in marriage but in providing me with the opportunity to obtain new clients. She was also an asset in maintaining the clients I already had. Phyllis, my wife, was as beautiful inside as she was physically. Her charming beautiful smile won people over before she ever spoke to them.

This case came to me as a result of Phyllis' friendship with a woman I will refer to as Marie. Marie and Phyllis often met for lunch or would go shopping together. Marie was the second wife of a gentleman I will refer to as Roger. On several occasions, the four of us would meet for dinner. I had only been with Roger and Marie on about three different occasions.

Roger was a nice enough guy, about 68 years of age. He was some 25 years Marie's senior. Roger had worked for a large specialty company with headquarters in St. Louis and retail stores over the entire United States. Roger had worked for over 40 years at a company, which I will refer to as Apex.

Roger had become one of the head buyers for various products sold by Apex with a buying budget of $20–25 million annually. Roger's buying trips would take him to New York, Miami, Chicago, Baltimore, and wherever there were products available to meet the requirements of Apex.

Apex had about six competitors throughout the U.S. Pricing was important for Apex in order to increase profits, which is true of every company. It was very rare that Roger was able to get much of an advantage over his competitors as they were generally all selling the same product and the advantage came with advertising, personnel, and store design. Every once in awhile, Roger would take advantage of a close-out or decide to buy larger quantities of several products that would be quoted at a lower price than the normal quantity purchased by his competitors. Roger supervised two younger assistant buyers in his department.

Being in a position to spend $20 million annually, the vendors would wine and dine the purchaser of their goods like Roger and his staff. Roger, however, was not interested in being taken out for dinner or given free tickets to a sporting event or a popular play on Broadway. Roger, it seemed, was all business and difficult to deal with. Roger insisted on getting the lowest prices from the vendors and more than once cancelled a large order when it was going to be several days late. Roger once threatened to stop doing business with a vendor when he discovered that a competitor purchased the same item for two cents per unit less. It did not matter to Roger that in that instance the vendor was selling the last of his 500 units with no guarantee of their condition and on a no-return basis. Roger was not well liked by his staff or the vendors, but he was very good at his job. Roger had informed his supervisor at Apex that he was going to retire at the end of the year, which would be December 31, 1975; however, the supervisor and the president of Apex convinced Roger to stay one more year so they could select his successor, whom Roger would help train.

Roger was paid a mere $75,000 annually, which was inadequate for someone with the responsibility for purchasing $20 million of product. Apex did have a good stock option plan and benefits, which included a pension plan for Roger and on his death, the payment would continue for Marie until her death. Roger was smart enough to pay more into his pension to protect Marie, which made the value of his pension in excess of $2 million since his wife was so much younger.

Roger had just completed a buying trip in New York, which lasted 4 days. He had met with about 20 different vendors and completed close to $7.5 million in purchases for the fall and winter seasons. The weather had been very hot in August when the trip took place. As usual, Roger rejected offers to dinner, plays, and the baseball game where the Yankees were at home against the Boston Red Sox. Instead, Roger spent each night alone in his hotel room planning for the next day's meetings with various vendors.

Roger returned home in late August satisfied that, as usual, he had completed a successful buying trip.

Roger was talking with his wife Marie shortly after that trip telling her how exhausting the buying trips had become and how glad he only had five more to do before he was to retire on December 31, 1976. Marie told Roger if it is so difficult he should tell the powers that be at Apex that he is going to retire this year and not stay the extra year. Roger said he had given the company assurances he would stay until they chose a replacement or December 31, 1976.

Unknown to Roger, Tony, an assistant to Roger for ten years, had met with the senior vice president of purchasing for Apex in late June 1975. Tony had no love for Roger and wanted his job. Tony told the senior vice president that Roger had been taking monetary kickbacks from the vendors Roger dealt with, which added up to a lot of money. Tony said he had proof from at least three vendors. Tony also said that these three vendors assured him that all the vendors made cash payments to Roger in order to do business with him. Naturally, Tony did not mention all the expensive dinners, shows, and sporting events he had received from these same vendors.

Apex had a rule about gifts to employees from vendors. The rule was simple: no employee can receive any gift in the value of more than $25 in any one-year period. This rule was in writing and sent to every vendor Apex dealt with. This rule was given to every employee and posted in various areas around the Apex offices.

Apex was a family-owned business now being run by the three children and grandchildren of the original founder. The head of Apex's legal department was married to one of the children and was an expert in money and rare coins. Martin Edes was his name and he was very bright and extremely ethical. He would frown on any employee not being as ethical as he, and would take all steps necessary to obtain all information available to determine if these allegations were true. If so, he would deal harshly with Roger, regardless of his long-term relationship with Apex, including the fact that Roger had an outstanding record as a buyer for Apex for over 25 years.

When the information from Tony was verified and the three vendors had signed affidavits under oath about giving money to Roger, the senior vice president met with Martin and several lawyers on the legal staff and presented the facts about Roger violating the company policy about gifts and taking kickbacks. Each of these vendors stated in the affidavit that they gave Roger an estimated $1,500 per year in cash in order to do business with Apex.

Martin was very angry when he read this report. He met with Tony and told Tony not to say a word but keep working with Roger and he would take over this investigation. It was about the middle of September 1975 when the chief legal counsel for Apex had sufficient cause to fire Roger for receiving kickbacks. Martin, however, wanted to know how extensive was this practice and he wanted a thorough and complete investigation.

Martin went to many of his legal contacts to find the best legal mind in the country to help guide Martin and Apex in this investigation. This cancer was invading the company for the first time in the history of Apex.

Martin felt that the leaders of Apex, from the founders to its current management, treated all of the key employees like family. These employees, Martin felt, had more than an adequate salary and bonus and their retirement benefits were exceptional in the industry.

Apex, with Martin's advice, hired Burt Robson, a well-known corporate attorney in New York, famous for handling a case of commercial bribery for one of the leading retail chains in the United States. In that landmark case, Robson obtained a large verdict against several companies that had provided expensive gifts including sums of cash and vacations to the buyers of this large national company.

Burt was retained in November 1975 and advised Martin that they should contact numerous companies Roger had dealt with and tell them that the management of Apex had been made aware of these cash payments to Roger and they wanted a full disclosure of any payments made. Burt also instructed Martin to advise these persons that if they did not come clean with the true facts of their dealings with Roger, their companies would be put on a Do Not Buy List and they would no longer do business with Apex.

This threat worked and another seven individuals who did business with Roger provided Apex with sworn affidavits that they gave Roger cash payments at his birthday, his anniversary, and at Christmas. These gifts varied from each company from $1,000 per year to $3,000 per year. All of these individuals were sworn to secrecy and Roger had no idea of the investigation.

Roger continued working as usual and was planning his next buying trip in February 1976. This unknown to Roger would be his last buying trip for Apex even though Roger had agreed to extend his date of retirement to December 31, 1976.

Apex formed a three-man committee to decide how to handle the termination of Roger after more than 40 years of service to Apex. Although Roger had done an excellent job for Apex as a buyer, Martin and two of the founder's grandchildren who made up the three-man committee to deal with Roger, felt betrayed and were angry. They decided that they needed to send a strong message to the employees of Apex, the business community, and all manufacturers providing goods to companies such as Apex that they would not tolerate the cash payments or gifts to the buyers of Apex or any Apex employee.

The investigation led by Burt Robson was completed by the end of February 1976 and they agreed to call Roger into Martin's office with Robson present to confront him about the evidence they had compiled regarding cash payments to him by the vendors.

What Burt Robson and the management of Apex did not consider was the new law regarding pensions, which became effective January 1, 1976. The acronym for this law is ERISA (Employment Retirement Income Security Act).

On the first Thursday in March 1976, Roger was summoned into Martin's large office. Seated at a small six-chair conference table was the president and senior vice president of Apex. These were two of the grandchildren of the founder. Also at the table was Burt, the New York expert who was leading the investigation.

Roger entered Martin's office around 4 p.m. and did not leave until a little after 6 p.m. As I found out much later, Roger had thought they were going to discuss some type of retirement gathering to honor his 40-plus years of service as Apex had done for previous forty-year employees who had retired.

Instead, Roger was greeted with accusations of his history of taking cash payments from the very persons he was empowered by Apex to purchase their goods at the lowest price possible. Roger vehemently denied any wrongdoing and insisted he had always obtained the lowest prices of any purchaser for the same product being offered by the vendors.

Confronted by the numerous affidavits signed by the vendors swearing they had made cash payments to him, Roger responded by simply admitting some vendors had sent him cash gifts at Christmas. None of these cash payments, according to Roger, influenced in any part his negotiations. Roger claimed he always received the highest quality of goods at the lowest price. Roger became angry at the accusation that he had done anything to the detriment of Apex and it was difficult for Roger to control his emotions. Roger was visibly shaken by the accusations being leveled at him by the very people he had been loyal to for over 40 plus years.

The outsider of the group, Burt Robson, saw this confrontation as a way to rekindle his fame as a leading authority on commercial bribery. It had been more than 10 years since Burt's big victory had been all over the trade papers and by now Burt remained in the shadows of great commercial litigators. Burt sensed this was his big opportunity to once again be recognized as the expert in the area of commercial bribery. As a result, Burt was focusing on bringing Roger to his knees and sure financial ruin.

In focusing on his own agenda, he spent his efforts trying to force Roger into admitting all of his illegal activities while dealing with the manufacturers he purchased goods from on behalf of Apex.

Burt convinced the Apex management to fire Roger immediately and to forfeit his pension, which was worth several million dollars. He also advised Apex to file suit against the five companies with the largest sales to Apex over the last five years and claiming damages of a minimum of the total amount Apex paid each manufacturer over that period plus punitive damages. The sales from the manufacturers totaled over $200 million during that time period. Apex would be required to file suit in New York, New Jersey, Illinois, Florida, and Maryland. The plan was also to sue Roger in St. Louis, but Roger was not made aware of that fact.

Toward the end of the meeting, Burt asked Roger if he would voluntarily authorize him to open Roger's safe deposit box that Roger kept at one of the large downtown banks, so they could inventory all of its contents.

Roger, by now, was exhausted and his face looked several years older than when he entered the meeting. Roger responded to this request by asking for a copy of this authorization to review and he would give them his answer by the end of the day tomorrow.

Roger left the meeting and drove home, but he had no recollection of doing that. During the entire thirty-minute drive, Roger was more concerned with how Marie was going to react to this news. Roger was aware of Marie's temper when things did not go her way. His immediate termination was bad enough, but the loss of his pension with payments to Marie after his death was devastating. Roger could not bear the tongue-lashing he expected to receive when he finally would get the courage to share this news with Marie.

Roger parked his car and slowly walked the fifty feet from the 2-car garage to the back door, which was his normal entry each day from work. As usual, Marie was seated in the den with her gin martini and reading one of the latest fashion magazines.

When Roger walked in, Marie, without looking up, asked Roger why he was home so late and further why had he not called to let her know he would be late. As Roger started to explain, his voice cracked causing Marie to abruptly turn and when she did, she looked at a man who looked worn out and very tired. Marie jumped up and went over to Roger very concerned and asked what happened. Marie thought one of Roger's children or fellow employees had been sick or worse.

Roger could not look Marie in the eye and with his face looking down toward the floor simply told Marie he had been fired. He did not tell her that they were not going to pay his pension, as she would find out soon enough. Marie also knew nothing of the cash payments her husband had been receiving throughout his employment as the buyer for Apex for over 40 years.

As Roger had anticipated, Marie was livid, however, not at Roger but at the Apex hierarchy whom he had given over 40 years of loyalty.

Marie had made plans with my wife, Phyllis, for the four of us to have dinner on Tuesday night, four days after Roger's termination. Knowing that I was an attorney, Marie had Roger call me the next day.

Roger simply told me in that brief phone call that he had been terminated by Apex after forty-plus years of service and he was accused of taking kickbacks, which he denied. I set up an appointment for Roger to meet with me the first thing Monday morning.

I had met Roger about three months earlier and had been to dinner with him and his wife Marie on just two occasions. I really did not know him very well, but he seemed nice enough and I was not sure that I would be able to help him with his problem.

On Monday, Roger arrived about ten minutes late. He had no documents with him. I had Roger take a seat at the small round conference table, which was large enough for four persons to sit comfortably.

It was my custom to interview clients at the conference table as opposed to having them sit across my desk, which is sometimes intimidating as my desk is usually covered with several files that I am currently working on and each would have two or three expansion folders. I did not want new clients to have a feeling that I was too busy to have time for their problems. As a result, my initial interviews would take place at the conference table which was always free from any clutter. In this way, the new client would always know that I am focused only on their issue. My receptionist is trained never to forward a call or interrupt me except for a real emergency when I am with a client.

The décor in my office is made to look like someone's living room. I have no wood paneling or diplomas or licenses on my walls. The wallpaper is soft and light and carpeting is deep and light colored as well. There are no file cabinets. It was my intent to have a client feel like they have come to my house and gone into the living room to discuss the client's problem.

As Roger started to discuss his problem, I immediately could hear the anger he was feeling. After 40-plus years of service to Apex, Roger was abruptly terminated for no good reason. He let me know that he had planned his retirement for December 31, 1975, but the management asked him to stay on one more year to help train his replacement, and out of loyalty to Apex, Roger did just that. In addition, Roger was upset that one of his assistants, Tony, was the one who first advised management that Roger was taking cash kickbacks from the manufacturers.

Roger let me know that he had never received any kickback from any manufacturer of goods he purchased.

Roger painted a picture of how competitive the sale of products Apex sold was around the country. Roger said he would never purchase any goods for a penny higher than one of his competitors. The merchandise being sold by Apex was exactly the same as was sold by its competitors for 80% of the merchandise. Roger advised if he paid more for the same exact merchandise as the competitor, then Apex would have to retail that same product at a price above that of its competitor. Roger's track record all those many years as a buyer was excellent and Apex always had a good profit margin on the goods Roger purchased.

Roger did admit that he had received cash gifts from various manufacturers at various appropriate times like his birthday or at Christmas. These gifts he said would be a couple hundred dollars. Roger went on to state that the other buyers at Apex accepted theater tickets and dinners to expensive restaurants but he never ever received those types of gifts. Roger said he was unaware of any other buyer receiving cash gifts such as he received. Roger also doubted whether any of the other buyers actually received kickbacks, which Roger interpreted to mean money in exchange for purchasing goods at a higher price than the true sales price per item.

What Roger failed to tell me is that Apex had a policy that no employee can accept gifts from anyone doing business with Apex with a value that exceeds $25. This policy was posted in many prominent places throughout the Apex offices. In addition, any person who did business with Apex was given a written copy of that policy at Christmastime. Roger then told me that he was asked to voluntarily allow Apex to open his safe deposit box to inventory its contents. They had provided Roger with an authorization to sign for that purpose and Roger said he would think about it and get back to them today. I advised Roger not to sign the form under any circumstances. I then asked Roger what he kept in that box. Roger assured me that other than documents such as the deed to his home, his birth certificate, and marriage license and some insurance policies, he had certificates for shares of stock he held in Apex and a few other stocks he owned. Even though the safe deposit box held nothing that could be construed negatively against Roger, I still advised him not to give Apex that authority.

I then discussed fee arrangements with Roger and told him that we could research the possibility into suing Apex for wrongful termination and other possible causes of action based on how the facts are developed. If in fact Apex refuses to pay his pension, we will have to sue in federal court, but not before we go through an administration hearing before the trustees of the Apex pension fund.

I then discussed fees with Roger and received firsthand knowledge of Roger being a very tough negotiator. What started out as an initial request for a $25,000 retainer at $200 per hour ended up with a very reluctant payment of a $10,000 retainer at $160 per hour.

I told Roger I knew one of the lawyers at Apex whom I could trust and see what their plans are as to his pension. This initial meeting lasted almost 3 hours.

That afternoon, I discussed the initial conference with Don Sherman, a younger lawyer who had just joined our firm two years earlier. Don graduated in the top three of his law class from Washington University in St. Louis. Don had practiced for two years after graduation with a very good firm but then he and his wife decided they would put their careers on hold and tour Europe for a little more than a year before settling down and starting a family.

Fortunately for my firm and me, I had learned that Don was coming back to St. Louis and was looking for employment as a lawyer. The person who first alerted me to Don's availability was my good friend and study group partner, Jerry. At the time, Jerry was an attorney in Apex's law department. Little did we know that Jerry's recommendation of Don would come back to affect Apex, Jerry's employer. Jerry was the lawyer I was referring to when I told Roger I was going to call a lawyer I knew who worked for Apex to find out what Apex intended to do in Roger's case.

Don and I concluded that if in fact Apex refused to pay Roger's pension, we could not file suit until we requested and had an administrative hearing with Apex. Don also would review the new ERISA law, but there had been so much publicity the six months before it became effective we were certain that Apex could not take away Roger's pension. There would be no legal cases we could rely on because the key issue had not yet been litigated. The issue was could an employer refuse to pay the pension of an employee if the employee had violated company policy. The answer to that question was much different after January 1, 1976, than it was prior to that date. Based on the voluminous amount of publicity being generated over the six months prior to ERISA becoming the "law of the land," Don and I felt pretty good about our chances to resolve the pension issue in Roger's favor; however, we knew it would not be easy both from an emotional and financial point.

Even before I had a chance to call my good friend Jerry, I received a phone call from Roger. This was just three days after our initial conference. Roger was very excited and let me know that he had been sued by Apex. He received a petition and summons and a writ of attachment on his safe deposit box.

I told Roger I would see him late this afternoon and to bring all of his papers with him, so we could review them together and discuss future steps we would need to take.

This time Roger, along with his wife Marie, were ten minutes early. I was able to see them right away, as my last appointment did not last as long as I had anticipated.

As Marie and Roger took seats at the conference table, I noticed there was tension between them. My secretary brought in the file which was still minimal, as not much activity had taken place in just a few days. Roger gave me the papers which had been served upon him that morning, and I handed them to my secretary and instructed her to make two copies and bring them back immediately so I could review them with my client and his wife.

As I took the time to review the Petition, which Apex had served Roger, I noticed something in this Petition much different than in most of the lawsuits filed against my clients. What caught my attention was, in addition to the Petition and Summons, there were additional documents rarely seen with the filing of a lawsuit.

Apex added an Attachment, which formally directed the bank where Roger had his safe deposit box to put a lock on the box, which prevented anyone from opening the box without an order from the Court. Attachment is usually used to recover assets after a judgment has been obtained. I had never in my career ever seen an Attachment of Assets used at the start of a lawsuit.

I was aware that an Attachment could be used prior to obtaining a judgment. In those instances, the moving party was required to put up a bond in an amount the judge deems reasonable. In this instance, no one but my client was aware of the contents kept in the safe deposit box. Only Roger would know the true value.

I immediately thought that I could possibly file a motion to dissolve the Attachment due to an insufficient bond. That thought quickly disappeared when I read the bond requirement required of Apex. They had been ordered to post a $1,000,000 bond before the Attachment was issued. I knew then that whatever Roger had in his safe deposit box one day would be revealed to Apex.

After I had finished reading the entire Petition and Attachment, I told Roger and Marie the basis of the lawsuit filed against Roger. In very simple terms, Apex alleged that Roger had violated company policy by accepting gifts in excess of $25 per year and these violations caused him to pay more than the normal negotiated rate per unit purchased from vendors. Apex alleged as damages the last five years of Roger's salary plus any bonus paid. In addition, Apex was claiming as damages the difference in the price per unit paid and the price that should have been paid to all vendors Roger did business with over the last 5 years. These damages could have added up to millions of dollars if Apex successfully could prove these damages.

I told Roger that we were going to be in a long and very expensive legal battle with Apex. I went on to advise Roger that he could no longer access his safe deposit box until the Court ordered it to be opened. Once again, I asked Roger what was in the safe deposit box. With Marie listening intently, Roger again stated only his important papers like birth certificates, warranty deeds, mortgage documents, and his shares of Apex stock.

I noticed that Roger was very agitated and Marie was extremely angry. She responded by loudly complaining about Apex being able to afford an expensive legal battle but they could not. She could not understand how Apex could seal Roger's safe deposit box without Roger knowing until he was served with the legal documents. I knew it would be a waste of time to explain the legal process to Marie as she seemed convinced that the system was rigged in favor of the wealthy. In some small way, she was correct.

After almost three long hours, our conference ended with Roger and Marie visibly angry, not just with Apex management but some of it directed at me. Not only could I not get Roger access to his safe deposit box, but he also had to write me a large check as my initial retainer to defend him in this lawsuit. In addition, I told Roger I would file suit in federal court to get the pension he earned after more than 40 years of employment with Apex. This could only be done after an administrative hearing with Apex.

I knew I had taken on a case with major legal issues, which involved defending a client who did not like paying any legal fees. Roger, I was sure, would be upset with the attorney's fees and costs he would have to pay not only to defend the case against Apex, but to also sue Apex for his pension benefits.

The suit for the pension benefits will be of national importance as it will be the first case filed under ERISA where an employee accused of violating company policy could be fired and still be entitled to his pension.

I was not prepared, however, for what came just 10 days after my initial conference with Roger. Apex had filed suit in New York, Florida, Illinois, New Jersey, and Maryland against each major vendor from whom Roger had purchased goods. In each state, Roger was named as a Defendant. Roger had been served at his home one night with five lawsuits and summons under the so-called "long arm" statute. This statute, which is almost identical in every state, provides that if an individual is doing business in a state, he subjects himself to the jurisdiction of that state. On the other hand, if an individual had been in the state on very limited occasions and was not regularly doing business in that state, there would be no jurisdiction on that individual.

In Roger's case, he had visited each of those states to meet with the principles of the vendor he was dealing with. The purpose was to be sociable with these persons and not necessarily do business, although on a few occasions some business was conducted.

Roger came into my office two days after he had been served with the five lawsuits. I had Don Sherman attend my conference with Roger. Don had shown early on an outstanding ability to comprehend all of the legal issues and the law that supported our position. Don had an excellent scholastic record from a prestigious law school. He had joined my firm three years earlier. I was very fortunate to have been able to hire such an intelligent lawyer with a load of pure commonsense.

The conference started with Roger spending about half an hour degrading and cursing each of the persons at Apex leading this charge against him. I allowed Roger to let off steam before I interrupted him and said we need to get facts from him in order to pursue the defense of these five lawsuits spread over five states.

Don took over the interview of Roger and advised him that it will be important to document his visits to each state in which he was sued. Roger was advised to get as many receipts as he could from each visit and be able to show he was not doing business in any of the states where Apex sued him. Don's plan for Roger was to file a Motion to Dismiss in each state on the legal grounds that the activity Roger generated did not rise to the level of doing business.

The Courts in each of these states, if they followed the law, would have to dismiss the lawsuit against Roger for lack of personal jurisdiction. Roger was aware if the Motion to Dismiss was lost in any one of the states the costs of his legal fees and expenses could escalate to a point where he could not afford to defend himself. Apex was hoping that would be the case.

When Roger left our office, he was angry and bitter over Apex's actions against him. Some of that anger and bitterness, although not verbalized, was directed at me and my firm because once again I had requested Roger write me another large retainer to cover the fees and costs in defending these five new lawsuits. Although Roger tried to negotiate a lower fee as he had done his entire career as a buyer dealing with Apex vendors, he finally reluctantly took a blank check from his pocket and wrote a check for the amount that was requested.

Just less than two months from the day I was retained by Roger, Don and I realized that we were litigating against Apex on three fronts. One was suing Apex in federal court in St. Louis to compel Apex to pay Roger's pension that would benefit both Roger and Marie after Roger's death. The value of that pension was in excess of several million dollars.

The second front was the defense of the five out-of-state lawsuits.

The third front was the defense of the claim for damages and return of Roger's salary for five years filed in St. Louis County Circuit Court.

Apex had retained Burt Robson, the New York attorney, to direct the legal strategy. Apex hired a large St. Louis law firm with over 100 attorneys to file the St. Louis County lawsuit and to defend the federal suit I had filed for Roger's pension. Apex hired a large law firm in each of the five states to bring suit against the vendor and Roger. In each of these five states I had to hire a local lawyer who would simply file a motion for pro hac vice to request our ability to litigate this one case as an unlicensed lawyer for that state. The local lawyer would vouch for our ability and the promise to follow all local rules. Usually we would pay $1500 to each local lawyer for this and agree they would have no other involvement in the case unless we lost our motion and Roger was forced to defend himself in any one of the five states.

Our law firm of twelve lawyers plus the five local lawyers we retained were greatly overshadowed by the 600-plus lawyers in the firms retained by Apex. This was truly a Sampson versus Goliath battle. If Vegas could have placed odds on our success in winning the five out-of-state cases for Roger, we would have been an underdog of huge proportions.

The Motions to Dismiss which we filed in each of the five states were mostly identical as the law we relied on was similar throughout the country. Personal jurisdiction over an individual is either that person resides in that state or a nonresident such as Roger does some activity that rises to the level of doing business in that state. The nonresident, by this activity, subjects himself to the jurisdiction of that state under the so-called "long arm statute." This simply refers to the state of New York or one of the other states in which Roger was sued, reaching into Missouri to serve Roger a summons and force him to defend himself in the state where he did not reside.

Don and I were under extreme pressure in defending Roger in the five non-Missouri suits. We both understood that a loss in any one of the out-of-state lawsuits would be devastating to my client.

Roger, now unemployed, was having to take money from his savings to pay the fees and expenses he was incurring. Roger and Marie lived very well. They had a large home in West County and dined out frequently. Marie dressed very well and each drove a very nice late model car. Now they were forced to get by on Marie's salary and Roger's Social Security. They did not receive enough money to meet their monthly expenses. Roger was getting more bitter as each month passed.

While Don was handling the out-of-state lawsuits, I was charged with the responsibility of filing suit in Federal court to force Apex to pay Roger his pension.

Before suit could be filed, I had to make a formal request to have a hearing in front of the Pension Board for Apex. The law required this type of hearing in order to prevent needless lawsuits and provide the employer an opportunity to correct an erroneous decision. In Roger's case, this hearing was a waste of time, as Apex had no intention of providing Roger his pension unless ordered to do so by the Court.

I prepared and sent the formal request for the pension hearing to the CEO of Apex by registered mail. In about 10 days, I received a formal response setting the hearing in two weeks. The location of the hearing was Apex's boardroom.

I advised Roger that he would attend the meeting but he would not speak. I planned to have a Court Reporter record everything that was said at that hearing.

Roger and I arrived about 15 minutes early for the 10 a.m. hearing. I gave my name to the receptionist located in Apex's lobby. We waited for approximately three minutes when a woman with a nametag, which read Helen, approached. She was about sixty years old and although, I later found out from Roger, she knew him as a fellow employee, Helen never acknowledged Roger's presence. She asked if I was Mr. Goffstein and I said yes and she said to follow her.

Roger and I were about five steps behind Helen and she led us to an elevator which took us to the 19th floor. As we exited the elevator, there were two massive oak doors opened and I was impressed immediately. There were large windows looking eastward with a full view of the Mississippi River. You could see barges going up and down the river. Inside the room was a group of men, all in suits and ties, milling around a very large conference table with red leather chairs. It appeared to me that there were 20 chairs, which were set 10 on each side of the table, and one chair at each end of the table.

It was interesting to note that not one of the gentlemen in the room looked at Roger nor did they attempt to speak to him. Every one of those men knew Roger very well and it appeared to me that they seemed uncomfortable. Roger was unusually quiet and he seemed to be gazing intently at everyone as if he were making certain they were aware of the bitterness he felt. From Roger's point of view, he was here to be punished for no reason after all those years of working for the success of Apex. It was as if he was betrayed by his fellow workers and the owners of Apex.

I did notice one friendly face in the crowd, my law school companion and my friend for over 30 years, Jerry. He came up and shook my hand and wanted to introduce me to Apex's legal strategist, Herb Robson. I left Roger alone and walked over to meet Herb. Jerry introduced me and explained to Herb our long friendship from high school, college, law school, and beyond. Herb Robson was about sixty-two or three with graying hair and about twenty pounds overweight. He wasted little time explaining how he was the country's leading authority on commercial bribery. He had represented a large national department store that sued vendors and the employee who took the bribes. The case was eventually ruled in the department store's favor and the employee as well as the vendors were hit with millions of dollars in judgments. Herb went on to say that the employee lost his pension for his actions. I asked Herb if that case was tried and he advised that the appellate decision in his client's favor was about nine years earlier.

Making sure I gave no edge to my opponent, I referred to him by his first name and made sure to remind him that his little victory was almost a decade ago and the laws have changed. Furthermore, I reminded Herb that he has not had me as the opposing counsel. I knew immediately, as did Herb, we would never be friends.

The hearing before Apex's Pension Board started on time. Three of the five members were new and were appointed just for this hearing. The three members the new appointees replaced were family of the founders of Apex. I insisted they be removed from Roger's hearing. Not wanting to be seen as biased, Apex agreed and added the new members. I was certain they had been instructed to vote to deny Roger his pension. The same instruction I am sure was given to the two non-family members.

The formal hearing went as planned. After all persons in attendance were identified on the record, I stood up and addressed the members of the Apex Pension Board.

I advised the Board that I had brought my own court reporter to record the entire proceedings. I then went through Roger's employment history with Apex, pointing out all of the excellent personnel reviews he had received over his 40-plus years. I went on to list each promotion he received working his way to the top as a senior vice president in the Purchasing Department. Roger had been an exemplary employee and yet Apex chose to ignore all his excellent work and deny Roger his pension on a false allegation of commercial bribery, I went on to say.

I paused for about a minute and the room was silent. None of the Pension Board members was looking at Roger or me. All had their eyes down and looking at blank notepads. Notes were not necessary when their "no" vote was already made. I took about 20 seconds to glance at the rest of the Apex officers seated about the boardroom and none would glance in my direction. That is, all except Jerry, my old friend, who had a strange look on his face. Maybe, I thought, Jerry is having second thoughts about initially acknowledging me as his friend when I first came into the Apex boardroom. It was obvious Roger was the enemy and anyone trying to help Roger was the enemy as well. Strangely, and much to my surprise, I was enjoying my new role. Although the pause was no more than 60 seconds, it must have felt like 60 minutes. I sensed an uneasiness that made its way into the boardroom and it was all on the Apex side.

I then spent the next 15 minutes explaining that as of January 1, 1976, ERISA was now the law of the land regarding vested pensions. I told the members of the panel that Roger categorically denies taking commercial bribes, but to make certain that this was not an issue in making their decision, I will, solely for the purpose of this hearing, admit Roger was accepting bribes in the form of cash payments from the vendors.

Even so, I went on to say, this panel, on behalf of Apex, could not deny Roger his pension. The law is clear that one who is vested in a pension plan cannot be denied that pension by the employer. That is the very purpose of ERISA. If you deny Roger his pension as you have been instructed to do, I said, then each of you individually as well as Apex will be sued in federal court. I reminded them that they could sue Roger in the state court of St. Louis County for damages which they had already done. I ended by urging the panel to do the right thing and follow the law: give Roger his pension that he earned. If you believe he did anything wrong to cause Apex damage, you can have your day in court.

When I finished, there was total silence. After about 45 seconds, the chairman asked if I had any witnesses. I replied that I have no more to present and sat down. The panel took a 15-minute recess and they left the room, as did the CEO and CFO of Apex. Herb Robson also left with them. Although my friend Jerry stayed in the boardroom, he made no effort to speak to me.

Roger turned to me and thanked me, but he looked very tired. Roger asked if there was any chance we could get Apex to change its position. I responded absolutely not. This is a vendetta against you for what they believe is a betrayal of their trust. They will use this matter to show all employees that if they do anything to harm Apex, then Apex will use its strength and financial resources to destroy that employee. I reminded Roger he is in a fight for his financial survival. The panel returned and the chairman adjourned the hearing saying we would receive their decision in a week.

As expected, the formal ruling was sent by registered mail to Roger's home with a copy to me. Unfortunately, Roger was not home when the letter arrived. Marie, as was her custom, opened all of the mail sent to the house and she opened the letter from Apex. Roger came home a few hours after Marie had read the letter from Apex denying Roger his pension. Apparently, Marie did not understand that Roger had zero chance of Apex agreeing to give Roger his pension. The hearing was a necessary step we needed to take before filing suit. Marie, however, was completely surprised by Apex's ruling. When Roger walked through the door, she started screaming at him nonstop for about thirty minutes for losing his pension and causing them to spend thousands of dollars in legal fees with no end in sight.

I opened my copy of the denial letter and was very pleased with the rejection by Apex of Roger's pension. Now I was able to file suit in federal court under the new ERISA law demanding Apex pay the full pension benefits to Roger and Marie if she is still alive after Roger's death. In addition, I demanded legal fees and costs for Roger incurred in this lawsuit.

My partner Don and I had already prepared the Complaint to be filed. Our plan was simple: as in the hearing before Apex, we admitted for the purpose of this lawsuit only, that Roger had violated Apex's policy by taking bribes from some or all of the vendors he dealt with as a buyer for Apex. We attached as exhibits the pension plan of Apex plus the last statement Roger received from Apex showing his benefits under the pension. In the petition, we cited the new ERISA law as the reason Roger was entitled to his pension.

It was Don's and my decision to proceed without the need to deny that Roger had taken bribes from vendors. Had we done so, this would have caused us to take numerous depositions from many out-of-state vendors that would have cost Roger a large amount of dollars for fees and costs that now would not be necessary. It took a two-hour meeting with Roger that this admission of wrongdoing would not affect any of the other cases and he was not bound in any manner by this admission. This was nothing more than a legal maneuver to get a quick ruling from the Court on the law. The facts would already be agreed to for this case only.

The suit was filed in the Federal court in the Eastern District of Missouri. We were assigned a federal judge who I knew from trying several cases in front of him both as a state court judge and a federal judge. Although this judge was not that great on the law, he had, as a clerk, a very bright older attorney who was a research genius and was in demand by all judges, both state and federal. I felt very confident that we would be successful in getting Roger his pension benefits, as the new ERISA law was that clear. In order to move matters more quickly, I sent a copy of the petition to Apex's attorneys and asked if they would waive personal service on their client, which they agreed to do.

Apex filed its answer with a list of affirmative defenses of all the violations of company policy committed by Roger.

In less than a week, I filed a response to Apex's affirmative defenses by simply stating: "For the purpose of this action only, my client will admit all the violations alleged in Apex's affirmative defenses." The response went on to state that even if my client committed all the violations alleged by Apex, they still must pay his pension benefits.

By the end of 8 days, I filed a Motion for Summary Judgment based on all the pleadings filed to date. There were no facts to be decided by a jury, as the facts were not in dispute. The MSJ, as the motion is referred to, simply asked the federal judge to apply the law to these facts.

Apex filed their response to the MSJ citing pre-ERISA cases, which were no longer relevant, but Apex had nothing else to support their position. I thought Apex's attorneys were hoping if they painted a picture of how bad a person Roger was the court would refuse to rule in Roger's favor.

I chose not to file a reply to Apex's response and as a result it was now up to the judge to make his ruling. I told Roger it could take several months for the judge to rule as this was a case of first impression and the Judge's opinion would be well drafted by his law clerk and could take some time to finalize.

About two weeks after our motions and memorandum of law were provided to the Court, I received the first good news for Roger. The judge in the New York case sustained our Motion to Dismiss as to Roger finding he was not doing business in the state and therefore not subject to their "long arm statute" and he was no longer a party to the suit in New York. One down and four to go, as I broke the news to Roger. I felt comfortable that we would be successful in the other four states, but not certain.

Within the next three weeks, the decisions from Illinois, Florida, New Jersey, and Maryland were received with the same result as New York. Naturally, Roger was ecstatic and feeling very good. I explained to Roger that none of these decisions as to his dismissal could be appealed until the entire case was completed, which could take years. With the five favorable opinions, Roger was now fighting Apex on just two fronts, which were his pension in the federal court and the suit in Missouri where Apex was suing him for damages.

Apex now started pushing hard on the Missouri case, apparently upset over the decisions that went against them. The attorneys filed a motion to unlock Roger's safe deposit box and inventory the contents. When I informed Roger of this, he became extremely angry and wanted to fight them to prevent this action. I was surprised by Roger's reaction but agreed to contest Apex's request, which I didn't think would be successful. In addition, this would be an added expense for attorney fees with no good result. Try as I could, Roger would not be content unless we opposed this Motion.

I filed the response to Apex's Motion to inventory the contents of Roger's safe deposit box stating it was premature as no judgment had yet been obtained and the contents were privileged and not relevant to any issues in the case. The Judge, who would preside over the case if it would be tried, heard oral arguments and ruled against my client. The Judge pointed out that the company had put up a million-dollar bond and if my client suffered any damages he could proceed against the bond Apex filed. Further, this is only discovery and although the contents may not be admissible at trial they were discoverable. The judge ordered the parties to agree to a date and time to view the contents within the next two weeks; if unable to agree, he would arbitrarily set a date and time. Roger was quite upset with this ruling and started accusing the Judge as being biased. There was no doubt that in Roger's mind, Apex's ownership had gotten to the Judge. I assured Roger this did not happen and the Judge's ruling was a correct one. I was surprised at Roger's reaction as there was nothing in the safe deposit box I was aware of that would affect my defense of the Missouri case. I even thought there could be a chance Apex would agree to allow Roger to sell his Apex stock; although if Apex agreed, I knew they would insist that the sale proceeds be retained either by the Court or in escrow until the Missouri case was completed.

I received a letter from Apex's attorney the next day, hand delivered, giving me three dates each at 2 p.m. to meet at the bank to open Roger's safe and inventory the contents. I contacted Roger and advised him of his options and he still was complaining of the Judge's bias. Finally, Roger chose a Friday date. I contacted Apex's attorney and advised him of the date chosen.

Roger agreed to meet me in the bank's lobby 15 minutes before 2 p.m. I arrived a half-hour before and went to the safe deposit box department and introduced myself to the vice president of the bank who would be handling the unlocking of Roger's safe deposit box. A few minutes later, Apex's attorney arrived with Martin, Apex's general counsel, and a court reporter. I noticed Roger walking through the lobby and I left the Apex group and went over to meet him. I advised Roger not to speak during this meeting but to take notes. I also advised him if he needed to take a break to let me know and we could discuss any issues he had during that time.

Roger and I then went to the vice president's desk joining the Apex attorney, their general counsel, and the court reporter.

The six of us then went to a large vault where the vice president walked us to Roger's box and with two keys unlocked the door and removed a fairly large box about 8 inches deep and 3 feet long. The vice president then left the vault with the five people following him into a small room with a small square table. He put the box in the center still unopened. The room was dimly lit with a small lamp at the end of the table. The court reporter set up his machine and the procedure started. First, everyone stated their names for the record and the vice president stated how he had removed the box from the vault and brought it to Room D unopened. It was agreed that the vice president would handle the contents in the box and identify each item for the record with each party representative having the right to comment on each item identified.

The safe deposit box was placed in front of the bank's officer and everyone was seated around the small table with all eyes on the unopened box. There was an eerie silence except for some heavy breathing that either was emitted from my client or the elder general counsel of Apex.

The lid of the safe deposit box of my client was lifted and when the full box was in view, I immediately felt my stomach turn and I was nauseous and slightly dizzy. I did everything to keep my composure and I made sure I did not turn to look at my client.

What I was looking at were stacks of $100 bills that had been originally wrapped with thick rubber bands. These stacks of money had evidently been in the box for a long time as each of the rubber bands had melted so they stuck to the top bill and had been split into several pieces. The bills, however, remained in good condition, having been out of circulation for a great number of years. Out of the corner of my eye, I noticed Roger turn away from the safe deposit box with his head gazed toward his feet. I realized that Roger had lied to me when we first discussed the contents in the safe deposit box. The irony of Roger not disclosing the money he had in the box was that there was a two-day window from the time he initially met with me and the date his safe deposit box was executed on by Apex. If Roger had advised me of this cash, I would have advised him to immediately go to the bank and remove this cash. We could make a decision as to how to handle this money at a later time. Now that option was gone.

The rest of the contents were what Roger had told me. There was the deed to his home, the mortgage, and note for his home, which had been paid in full, and birth certificates. Martin, Apex's general counsel, was a numismatist and requested the right to look at the $100 bill on top of each stack. It turned out there were 23 stacks of bills with 100 bills in each stack totaling $230,000. Martin, on the record, was able to cite the date the bill was printed and the location.

The entire process took a little less than two hours. As we left the bank together, Roger wanted to explain the money in the box. I was so angry I just looked at Roger, unable to hide my disgust, and said this is not a good time for us to talk and he should call me in a few days while I think about today's events.

As I drove back to my office, I knew that the chance of successfully defending Roger in the Missouri case was less than fifty percent. I knew that somehow I needed to try and settle the case, but that would not be easy. Apex was out for blood, Roger's, and Roger still believed he had done nothing wrong.

As I drove back to the office, I thought about the fact I had a client who was angry at me for charging him what he believed were too much in attorney fees and in addition he couldn't be trusted. To go along with Roger, I had to deal with his wife Marie, who hated the fact that her lifestyle had to change because of the fees being paid to our firm.

The experience at the bank brought me way down from the high I felt when we won the Motions to Dismiss in the five states. I was still anxiously waiting for the Court's ruling on our Motion for Summary Judgment for Roger's pension. It had been almost two months since all briefs had been filed.

After the episode at the bank, things started heating up, as Apex scheduled Roger's deposition not only for the Missouri case, but for the other cases where Apex sued the vendors.

Roger's deposition for the Missouri case was set about three weeks after the bank meeting. I met with Roger a week before his deposition was scheduled to prepare him for the questions he would be forced to answer as to how he acquired all the cash found in the safe deposit box. I was also interested to know the facts about this money, but I doubted Roger would give me a truthful answer. In over roughly a four-hour session, the story that Roger provided was going to be very difficult to use to convince a jury. However, it was the best I was given by my client.

According to Roger, every buyer at Apex violated the $25 gift rule and upper management was well aware of that fact. Every Apex buyer is wined and dined by every provider of Apex. They are given theatre tickets, along with birthday and Christmas gifts. Roger estimated the value could be anywhere from $250 per buyer to $2000, depending on the level the buyer has reached with Apex, along with the budget the buyer controlled. According to Roger, he averaged about $1800 per year from each of the manufacturers he did business with, and he did business with at least 40 vendors each year.

Roger further stated that he did not trust anyone enough to confide in regarding these cash gifts, including his first and current wife. Roger went on to state that he started stacking the bills into $10,000 stacks and wrapped each with a thick rubber band. He occasionally would use the cash to pay his restaurant bills on those places he frequented and also to pay the bills of department stores his wife frequented. Most of all, he saved this money for his retirement. Roger was adamant that not once did he compromise Apex on his buying trips. Roger went on to state that he always paid the lowest price for the goods he purchased. Roger explained that Apex's competitors were many, and if he had paid the vendors a higher price, then the goods he purchased could not be sold at a competitive price and Apex's profits would diminish. Roger did not have any regrets about violating Apex's policy of accepting gifts in excess of the $25 value because everyone was doing it.

As I listened to Roger explain his position, I felt his story would not be accepted by a jury. Roger would not make a good witness, as he would lose his composure when he was examined on the cash he was receiving from all the vendors and the large stacks of $100 bills in his safe deposit box.

I was aware that at this time early in the Missouri litigation, it would be useless to discuss with Roger for him to consider settlement with Apex.

Finally, after almost three months, the Federal court issued its ruling on our Motion for Summary Judgment regarding Roger's pension. The Court, in an 18-page opinion, not only awarded Roger his pension, but also ordered the Court to hold an evidentiary hearing to decide the amount of attorney's fees Apex should pay Roger for having to file the lawsuit.

Finally, there was good news to report to my client. This decision was a real blow to Apex. When I told the good news to Roger, he was elated. He asked when he could start receiving his pension benefits, as well as the back benefits due. He was disappointed when I said that Apex will appeal the decision to the U.S. Court of Appeals, and it may be another eight months before we have the final decision. Roger was disappointed and blamed the judicial system for this delay. Roger's opinion would have been different had he lost the case at the trial level and became the appellant.

As if I were a psychic, just as I predicted, Apex filed its appeal with all the required paperwork. Apex would have to file its brief and we would file our response brief. Apex would file its reply brief and then the appellate court would set a date for oral argument. After the argument, it could take anywhere from two months to five months for a decision.

Now as the litigation was winding down, the only trial left was the case set in St. Louis County. Roger had won the five out-of-state cases and the pension case, although that was not yet final. Apex spent the next several months taking depositions of vendors. I took the depositions of many of the buyers from Apex, as well as the management team.

The buyers for the most part admitted receiving theatre tickets and dinners from the vendors. I could not get one to admit he received cash from any vendor.

Each buyer I deposed admitted the dinners and theatre tickets exceeded $25, but all of them testified that this did not violate the $25 rule imposed by Apex. They all testified that this was entertainment and not a gift as the Apex policy referred to. I felt that Apex would have a difficult time differentiating the dinners and theatre tickets from the $25 rule they imposed. I believed I could convince a jury that all the buyers were violating this rule and as a result, Apex never enforced this rule. My problem was convincing a jury that the large amount of cash in the safe deposit box was acceptable as a gift and not a bribe.

I also felt that Apex would have a difficult time proving they were damaged by Roger's acceptance of the money from the vendors.

If Roger truly purchased the vendors' goods at the lowest prices and the quality of the goods was the same as sold to other vendors, then the attorneys for Apex would have a difficult time proving they suffered any damages.

After all pretrial discovery had been completed, the court set a status conference to see if the case could be settled and, if not, set a trial date.

About a week before the status conference, I was sitting in my office when my receptionist advised me that I had a call from Stan Hartman. Although I had no idea who the caller was, I told my receptionist to put him thru. My phone rang and as I put the phone to my ear and said "hello," the next words I heard were one of the most exciting of my life. Stan's words were "Mr. Goffstein, this is Stan Hartman from the Department of Labor, Washington, D.C., and we want to file a brief in support of your position with the Court of Appeals."

Stan and I talked about thirty minutes. He said my case had the set of facts they were looking for to support the proposition that ERISA was passed to protect an employee's pension once the employee was vested. This was true even if the employee violated company policy or committed a crime. The employer could not take away a pension once vested.

He requested that I send him my research that supported my legal position, and he would send me a copy of the government's brief before it was filed. This was known in the legal community as an amicus curiae meaning a "friend of the court."

Now I was really excited. Not only did I have the law on my side, but I now had the U.S. Department of Labor arguing my position. My client was happy upon hearing the news, but frustrated that he had no money from his pension.

The next week I appeared at the status conference in front of Judge Stark. I had known the judge for many years, first appearing before him as an associate circuit judge early in my career. He was very practical and fair. The two local attorneys for Apex were there, but no clients, as settlement would seem impossible based on the personalities of the Apex management and my client.

The judge started the conference asking if settlement discussions had taken place or does this case have to be tried. I responded by saying I think the attorneys could talk settlement, but this is personal to both my client and Apex.

I asked the lead attorney if he was aware that the Department of Labor was going to file a brief supporting my client, and of course he had received the motion requesting leave to file their brief. We talked about the law, which supported my client's position for receiving his pension, and Apex's lawyer did not disagree, but still would not agree that I was going to win the pension case. It appeared that Apex's lawyer was not as aggressive as he had been initially.

I told the judge that, in my opinion, even if the jury found Roger had violated Apex's policy of receiving gifts over a value of $25, Apex could not prove damages. The judge asked Apex's lead counsel on the issue of damages and the facts that supported the company's claim. The attorney responded that their expert had not completed his report, but they believed the damages could be close to $1,000,000.

The judge set the trial for a date almost three months past our status conference.

I was having mixed feelings about the two cases I was handling for Roger. I felt extremely comfortable on the pension case, but I was very uneasy about successfully defending the commercial bribery case.

As things developed, the Department of Labor filed its brief and oral arguments were heard, all before the trial date in state court. Then, due to a conflict, Judge Stark extended the trial date two more months.

About two weeks before the trial date before Judge Stark, I received the appellate court's decision. As I had expected, they affirmed the District Court's decision awarding Roger his pension and directing the trial court to have a hearing on awarding my attorney's fees. Even though I expected this ruling, I was excited, as I knew what a victory this had been for Roger. We had taken on the establishment with all of its influence and money to hire the largest law firms with the best reputations and won.

I called Roger and told him the news. He was truly excited for the first time. I told Roger there would be a hearing on my attorney's fees and after the ruling on my fees, Apex would need to decide whether or not to appeal. I was not sure whether or not Apex would appeal this ruling because the next court to hear this case would be the Supreme Court of the United States. Selfishly, I would welcome the opportunity to argue a case before the highest court in the land, but for my client's sake, the litigation needed to be over. It had been going on for over three years and had cost my client a lot of money, and he had yet to receive one cent.

The case in front of Judge Stark was set for Monday and Roger and I had spent the previous four weekdays preparing him for trial. We had gone through all his testimony he had given in numerous depositions in all the out of state cases, as well as the Missouri case. On Friday, I told him to get plenty of rest over the weekend, as he will be facing a very difficult trial that could last seven or eight days.

I would be spending the weekend preparing my exhibits and reviewing my outlines of all depositions I had taken of the Apex employees plus the depositions of the various vendors. My weekend would be spent in the office with my partner, Don, and two associates getting ready for trial.

On Saturday afternoon around 2 p.m., I received a call from Roger stating he needed to see me immediately. He said he just received a registered letter from the IRS. Roger sounded very upset, and I told him to come to the office as soon as he could.

Roger arrived in about 20 minutes and was visibly shaken. He sat across my desk and reached into his pocket and handed me a folded envelope, which had obviously been torn open at one edge. I reached into the envelope and removed the letter. As I unfolded the letter, I could see the words "Internal Revenue Service." As I slowly read the letter and re-read it a second time, I finished and then handed the letter over to my partner, Don, who had a quizzical expression. I did not make any comment to Don, but I wanted him to review the letter without my thoughts, which might influence his opinion.

I turned to look at Roger who had a bewildered expression as if to say, "What the hell is going on?" No one spoke for at least ten minutes. The silence was deafening. It seemed like hours had passed before I finally spoke. I waited until Don put the letter down and nodded, indicating he understood the letter's significance.

I started my discussion advising Roger that the registered letter from the IRS was a game changer as far as the defense of our case with Apex. I told Roger that we could no longer litigate the Missouri case with Apex, as this letter makes it impossible to do so. As I discussed the letter from the IRS, I pointed out the obvious. The IRS had decided to bring a criminal indictment against Roger for unreported income. They obviously were aware of the large amount of cash found in Roger's safe deposit box.

Although I could not prove it, someone at Apex's direction was giving the deposition testimony Roger had given in all those cases to the IRS. The IRS had the manpower and resources to spend hundreds of thousands of dollars bringing criminal charges against Roger. Roger had no such resources to defend himself even if he could prove he did not commit any criminal act.

I explained to Roger that he was given one chance to request a hearing with the IRS to try to convince them not to proceed with criminal charges. This hearing must be requested within 60 days from the date of the letter, which gave us 57 days. I told Roger that the IRS would attend the trial and monitor every word. The best Roger could hope for, I told him, was that we make a reasonable settlement with Apex and then try to convince the IRS to drop the criminal action. In my opinion, we had a 70 percent chance of settling the Apex case and a 10 percent chance to convince the IRS to drop the criminal charges.

I appeared in Judge Stark's courtroom at 8:30 Monday morning, as the judge had requested. Jury selection would not take place until after 10:30, as the jury pool would be chosen around 10 a.m. from the jury room.

Then the panel would be brought down to the third floor where Judge Stark's courtroom was located and wait outside until the judge was ready to proceed with voir dire, which is picking the jury, who will decide the case.

Apex's two attorneys arrived shortly after me and we advised the clerk that the attorneys were ready to meet with the judge to take care of preliminary matters. These preliminary matters would be to discuss the number of jurors needed on the initial panel, the instructions to be given to the jury after the close of the case, and any last minute legal issues either party needed to discuss.

The judge had set aside eight days for trial. Based on my past experience with Judge Stark, he was not anxious to sit for eight days for one trial. He knew a lengthy trial created legal issues, as he would have to rule on all legal matters raised and there could be many. He was also aware of the emotional feeling on both sides. I felt Judge Stark would listen to any suggestions from either side that could get this matter settled.

The Sunday before trial, I made a decision to advise the judge about the letter my client received from the IRS. I was aware this would be shared with Apex's counsel, but I was fairly certain they had already been aware of this information. I was pretty sure that Apex's owners had insisted on going to the IRS with information of Roger's cash in the safe deposit box.

As we started the discussions in the judge's chambers as to preliminary matters, I told the judge that I had another issue to discuss first and it would take about 15 minutes. There was no objection from Apex's attorneys.

I went on to inform everyone, off the record, meaning no court reporter present, of the IRS letter intending to bring criminal charges against my client. I further stated that my client, as well as his wife, have no intentions of offering any money to settle this case. I then requested time to persuade my client to settle this case, and it could take all day. I suggested the judge continue the case until Tuesday and let me try and get settlement discussions going with Apex. Without objection from Apex's attorney, the judge entered an Order to continue the case until 9:30 a.m. on Tuesday.

I then went back to the courtroom where Roger was waiting alone. His wife, Marie, he said, could not bear to sit through the trial. I knew that would not be helpful if we could not settle the case.

I told Roger of my plan to attempt settlement and he became irate. He was not going to give those SOB's one penny. That was the reaction

I expected, and I responded by advising Roger that I wanted him to just listen and make no statements until he heard and understood what I was attempting to accomplish. Roger calmed down and just glared at me without saying another word. I advised Roger I was first going to meet with the attorneys for Apex.

I went to Apex's attorney and said I would hope to get a settlement figure from my client without Apex making a demand. This was unusual to say the least, but I was aware that Apex's demand would be so high, I would never get Roger to respond. In the legal world, this is "bidding against yourself" and is never done, but I felt the circumstances of this case called for unusual tactics in negotiating.

I told the attorneys that I was going to try to convince my client to make a settlement offer that would be substantial, but nowhere near the demand of Apex. I also told them their major obstacle would be proving damages, as not one witness who had been deposed testified that that they charged Apex a higher price than any other company for the exact same merchandise. As a matter of fact, Roger purchased some of the same goods at a slightly lower price in over 45 percent of the purchases. I agreed the cash in the safe deposit box would hurt my client. I also acknowledged that the threat of criminal prosecution was a game changer.

I then left the courthouse with my client and picked a nice Italian restaurant for lunch. It was a two-block walk to the restaurant and my client could not stop talking about not paying one dime to those no good SOB's. He kept saying how he gave them over 40 years of his life and this is how he is treated. I pretended to listen, as we walked for about 15 minutes not saying a word, but thinking how am I going to convince my client to settle this case?

When we arrived at the restaurant, my favorite dining place, I told the waiter to sit me at my usual table and bring two vodkas on the rocks. I knew I needed one and was sure Roger would not object.

During the initial thirty minutes, I just listened, as Roger railed against Apex, the judicial system, and my extremely expensive legal fees. He felt he had gone through hell with all of the legal cases he had to face, and he had been wronged by the very people he had worked so hard for. After he had consumed the first drink and took as few sips from the second drink, his mood changed. His tone was softer and his body less tense. He was enjoying his salad and pasta. He paused for about a minute, which gave me an opportunity to discuss my plan for a possible settlement.

I had prepared for this moment by retaining an excellent tax attorney, Sanford Pomerantz, to advise me as to all the tax benefits of my plan, as well as the slim chance of getting the IRS to drop the criminal charges. I started by explaining to Roger the cost of trying this lawsuit to conclusion, as well as the appeal which would certainly come no matter who won the trial. I estimated the eight-day trial would cost him in the range of $150,000 and an appeal another $50,000. I went on to state that there was a 70 percent chance we would lose the case and a jury would award the amount found in his safe deposit box plus an additional sum for either damages or punitive damages, which could total about $500,000. Using the 70 percent chance of losing the case, I attributed $350,000 to the judgment.

I kept my eyes directly on my client's face to see any signs of him understanding the consequences of going to trial, and this was without considering the impact of the IRS criminal charge, which was significant.

For the first time, I became aware that Roger was starting to realize the gravity of his situation. He stopped sipping on his drink and pushed aside his food and was apparently hearing what I was saying.

I continued my discussion by going through a plan to have the settlement funds to offer Apex. I reminded Roger that when this suit was filed against him and his safe deposit was sealed, we wrote Apex advising we would sell his stock in Apex and we wanted it released, which Apex refused to do. In the almost three years while the stock was in the safe deposit box, the stock almost doubled in value. Roger could sell 50% of the stock if we settled the case and, after capital gains tax, realize almost $280,000. The stock he had left had a value of slightly more than the value on the date the box was sealed.

I said to Roger that if there was an omen from a higher power, this is a great example. The higher power was giving him a way out and he should pay attention. I noticed Roger's body seemed to be more relaxed and a smile very faint started to appear. I was not sure if it was the settlement strategy I was presenting or the alcohol he had been drinking. Either way, my discussions of settlement seemed to be taking root.

I went on to explain to Roger that Apex refused to pay him dividends on the stock he owned and over almost three years, the dividends total almost $35,000. I said we could offer to give this money to Apex, along with the funds from the sale of the stock, which now would total $315,000. I reminded Roger that the dividends, if he received them, would be taxable and he was not personally giving up the full $35,000.

The next part of my plan was going to be a tougher sell, and I knew I had to be certain I presented it in the right way in order to convince Roger it was the thing to do. I went on to explain to Roger that the cash in his safe deposit box was something that the owners of Apex could never forgive. Those packets of $10,000 in $100 bills were like salt on an open wound. I told Roger that he had to forfeit some of that money to Apex as a sign that he had violated their gift policy and was willing to pay a penalty from those gifts. I suggested if we pay them $100,000 from the cash and the $280,000 from the sale of the stock and call it return of salary as a result of this violation of their gift policy, this would be tax deductible and it would not cost him the full $380,000, as at least 35 percent of the payment would be deductible. This tax information came from my retained expert, Sanford Pomerantz, and I was confident of the validity of his advice.

By this time, it was almost 4 p.m., and nearly four hours had passed. I told Roger to go home and discuss my plan with Marie, and we would meet tomorrow at 9:30 a.m. in Judge Stark's court to negotiate with Apex's attorney.

The next morning, I had already planned to meet with the judge and Apex's attorney at 9 a.m. in the judge's chambers. I advised Judge Stark that I had discussed settlement with the client and he was willing to consider a reasonable settlement since he is aware of the legal fees and costs he would incur if this matter goes to trial and a jury verdict, as well as the appeal, which would be inevitable.

Apex's lead attorney said his client also is willing to discuss settlement, but as he put it, the amount had to be substantial enough to send a message to all employees of Apex that you do not violate Apex's policy on accepting gifts. Apex's attorney seemed more conciliatory as ever before, and I felt settlement was possible. The judge agreed to give us a full day for the second time to try to achieve a settlement.

When we left the chambers and entered the courtroom, I saw Roger in the back row reading the paper. Roger looked very tired, as if he had been up all night. My guess was that he and Marie had some heated discussions on my settlement scenario.

I sat down beside Roger and told him I would be meeting with Apex's attorney in the lawyers' lounge and he should stay close by so we could discuss the ongoing negotiations. I then went to the lawyers' lounge and Apex's attorney was waiting. He had removed his jacket and loosened his tie and had a pad and pen laid out. I sat down across from him and started the settlement discussions.

I started the conversation with the fact that the pension issue has been resolved for the most part by the ruling of the Court of Appeals. I told him that, in my opinion, his client does not wish to appeal this case to the Supreme Court of the United States and receive all the negative publicity that would follow. I went on to state that I was aware my client had truly pissed off Apex's owners and want Roger punished.

I told Apex's attorney that my major concern for my client was the IRS threat of criminal prosecution, not because of any guilt on Roger's part, but the cost of defending such a case would cost several hundred thousand dollars. I went on to make my initial offer of $250,000 with the condition that three years of salary is being returned for violating the company's gift policy. That amount was $225,000. Naturally, Apex's attorney said the amount was not acceptable as too low, but he would convey his offer to his client and get back to me within the hour. This information of getting back to me that quickly was a good sign. I now was pretty sure Apex wanted to end this litigation. The unknown was how much would it cost my client and also could I keep my client under control.

I went back to the courtroom where Roger was waiting. I told him of my initial offer to Apex and the fact that we should receive a counter demand in about an hour.

While we waited, I advised Roger that I had sent a registered letter to the IRS demanding a conference to attempt to persuade them from proceeding with the criminal charges. I was hoping they would respond with a date for the meeting, which would be acceptable with my schedule. I again emphasized to Roger that we needed to settle this case with Apex. He should not testify.

I then told Roger he needed to contact every manufacturer he dealt with and have each one sign an Affidavit, which I would prepare. My plan was to convince each manufacturer Roger located to sign an Affidavit under oath that admitted giving Roger money each year was a gift. I also needed each one to state that they never took a deduction for these gifts. I explained to Roger the importance of proving that the gifts were not earned income, and the government was not out any money because of deductions. I told Roger if he became aware one of the buyers he previously dealt with had died, try and get some confirmation from a family member of that person's death by requesting a note to that effect. Over the years, Roger had dealt with over sixty manufacturers. I told Roger it was necessary he spend the next few weeks working on this, as it would be extremely important to try to convince the IRS to drop the proposed criminal charges.

Roger thought he could get a number of the buyers to sign such an Affidavit, as he had kept in touch with many of them during the course of the litigation with Apex.

I then noticed that Apex's lead attorney was outside the courtroom in the hall. I left Roger and went out to talk with Apex's attorney. We went up to the lawyer's lounge and sat at a table in the corner at the back of the lounge. We helped ourselves to the complimentary beverage and some snacks and then Apex's attorney began the conversation.

First, he said the offer of $250,000 was rejected. He went on to state that Apex was willing to settle, but management insists Roger cannot profit from his actions and he must pay a price. Apex's officers believed that Roger, by accepting money as he did, poisoned the system that up to now had relied on good-faith, arms-length, bargaining.

Apex's attorney went on to state they wanted Roger to pay $750,000 and they would agree to accept part of that sum as return of salary. I immediately thought that I now have an excellent chance of settling this case with Apex. The only issue was how much. I also discussed the fact that I believed Apex representatives put the IRS on Roger and that did not make Roger eager to pay Apex any money, especially as he would need the funds to defend himself. I went on to state that I would consult with Roger and hopefully come back with a counter offer. At this point, Roger and Apex were one-half million dollars apart.

I went back to meet with Roger in the empty courtroom. As I came in, I noticed Roger looking older than his 70 years and staring at the ceiling as if he were looking for relief from above. Roger turned when he heard me come in and walked hurriedly toward me. He first said, "Can we get this damn thing over with today?" I took Roger's arm and took him back toward the counsel table and sat him down.

The good news, I started off, is Apex will discuss settlement. The bad news is their demand is $750,000, and we are only one-half a million dollars apart. Roger did not smile. I told Roger the hard part was getting Apex to agree to settle. Now, I said, we need to be creative and find a way to satisfy you and at the same time satisfy Apex. A good resolution is when neither side is happy with the results. The payor complains he paid too much, while the payee complains he did not receive enough.

I started to work with numbers on my legal pad, all the while listening to Roger complain bitterly about paying one dime to Apex. I mostly ignored Roger, as I did not want to have to convince Roger a second time that he had no other options than to try to settle this case.

I started with the cash in the safe deposit box. There was about $230,000 in the box. If we used $130,000 of that money and gave up the dividends of about $35,000, we had $165,000. If we then returned the stock certificates to Apex without selling them, the value before any capital gains tax would be approximately $360,000, and Roger would retain stock in Apex totaling about $390,000. I could now present a package to Apex totaling $525,000 without considering tax issues. How to pay that money was going to be an issue. I wanted to now make the return of salary five years. This meant that $375,000 of the payments would be tax deductible to Roger and cost Roger approximately $285,000. I thought it would be important to Apex that Roger was going to return a large amount of the cash in the safe deposit box.

I now had a plan which made sense to me, but it was not my money. I had to first convince Roger and, if successful, convince Apex.

I asked Roger if he would like to go outside and walk around the local park a couple of blocks from the courthouse. It was now about 3 p.m., and the sun was shining with the temperature a delightful 75 degrees. As we were walking, I talked about the cost of litigation for both the Apex case and the IRS criminal case if I were to be unsuccessful in convincing the IRS to drop the criminal charges. I went on to state the obvious, which was that a loss to Apex would only cost Roger money, but a loss to the IRS would not only cost Roger money, but possibly as much as six years of his freedom. I could only emphasize that gambling with money is a lot easier than gambling with one's freedom. I went on to remind Roger that the two trials would cost him a lot of money for fees and costs, even if he were to be successful in both cases.

Roger and I walked for more than an hour. We found ourselves back at the courthouse and stopped. I put my hand on Roger's shoulder and turned him so we were facing each other and I said, "Roger, I need to know if you want me to end settlement talks and start the trial with Apex or end this litigation and use our resources on the IRS." Roger just looked at me for about a minute without saying a word and then softly said, "Just settle it." Roger looked more sad than angry. I believe he finally realized either decision he would make would cost him a lot of money. I also think that he now realized the chance of him spending the last years of his life in prison was possible.

My goal was to settle the Apex matter as I had outlined to Roger within the next day. I would then focus all my energy on the IRS issue.

I told Roger to go home and I would meet Apex's attorney in the afternoon and hopefully have this matter resolved.

I left Roger and called Apex's attorney to have him meet me in the chambers of Judge Stark at 4:30 p.m. I then went to see Judge Stark and advised him that I had my client's permission to make a fair offer to settle the case and Apex's attorney would be present at 4:30 p.m. I requested the judge to help us resolve this case, and that I would need at least a third day to try to settle this matter. The judge agreed to continue this case another day, as it was in everyone's interest to achieve a settlement since a trial would be lengthy, expensive, and any jury verdict would be appealed.

When Apex's attorney came into the chambers, Judge Stark asked him to close the door. The judge picked up his phone and told his clerk he did not want to be disturbed. It appeared Judge Stark was prepared to stay late to help resolve this case.

I told Apex's counsel that my offer was going to be the most money my client would pay. The key to settlement is how to designate the payments. First, I said the package will total approximately $525,000. Of this amount, $360,000 will be the value of Apex's stock my client will forfeit to Apex. In addition, my client will forfeit dividends due him that total about $35,000. Lastly, I said that Apex's owners will be happy to know Roger would give them $130,000 of the cash found in his safe deposit box. Apex should be thrilled that my client is giving up money that they believe constituted commercial bribery. I ended my settlement negotiations with the attorney for Apex by letting him know that I had used all my ability to get my client to agree to part with this sum of money. Much of the money needs to be tax deductible in the five-year return of salary plus the tax savings by forfeiting dividends and return of Apex stock. Finally, I said, if this is rejected, my client and I are prepared to go to trial.

Apex's attorney said he would meet with the decision makers this afternoon and have an answer by noon tomorrow.

Judge Stark listened to my offer and agreed to delay calling a jury for a third day while we continued to finalize a settlement. This three-day delay of calling for a jury was unprecedented in my career, but the judge's patience was necessary to reach such a settlement.

I left the judge's chambers and met with my client and briefed him on what had been offered. I told him if the offer were accepted, we would sign documents which formally showed the case was passed for settlement with amounts being paid. The details of the settlement would be put in a document referred to as a Release of All Claims, which would cover all the finer points of the settlement at a later date. I went on to tell Roger if Apex did not accept our offer, we would probably be ready to pick a jury on Thursday and start opening statements on Friday after the jury selection.

Roger said he would tell Marie about the settlement offer only if it were accepted. I was not sure this was a good idea, but I was not going to persuade Roger to tell her now. I had already put much needed pressure on him to make the offer he did. I thought maybe it was better for him to have a quiet evening and not think about the case until we heard from Apex.

The next morning, I received a call from Apex's attorney stating his clients have not rejected the offer, but are considering the tax consequences of accepting five years of salary, the return of stock, and forfeiture of dividends. The other issue was the hearing set in the next two weeks on my attorney's fees from the pension case. I told Apex's attorney that my fees in the pension case are not part of the settlement discussions for this case. As for the tax consequences for Apex on the settlement funds, they would need to resolve this without my input. I just needed to know their final decision as soon as possible, as I had to face the IRS with the tax issue once I got this case settled. I went on to state that I was not sure how long

I could control my client and keep the offer open. There was a chance if too much time passed, Roger could withdraw his offer.

I called Roger and advised him that it appeared Apex was seriously considering our offer and they needed more time to consider the tax issues, if any, on how they receive the money from him by way of stock and dividends. Roger seemed to be nervous and I asked him if he told Marie about the possible settlement yet. Roger replied that unless there was something definite, he did not want to unnecessarily have to deal with Marie.

It was not until almost 3 p.m. when I heard back from Apex's attorney. His clients had agreed to the terms of the settlement offer and they would insist on having the money within 30 days. I immediately agreed to the 30 days, provided it was from the date all settlement documents were signed and the dismissal with prejudice was filed. He agreed and we discussed meeting in the courtroom and drawing up a memorandum of settlement and having Roger sign it along with Apex's representative.

I called Roger and told him the case was settled and to meet me in Judge Stark's courtroom in the next thirty minutes. I was excited for my client, but did not believe from the sound of his voice that Roger shared my excitement.

I met Apex's attorney in the courtroom. He had written a memorandum of settlement for the clients and attorneys to sign, as well as signature for the judge. Except for a couple of minor changes, I felt the memorandum described the settlement I proposed. The Release, which would follow, would be more detailed.

I showed the memorandum to Roger who read it quickly and then signed above his typed name. Sitting across the table was Apex's vice president of sales who at one time was a friend of Roger's. Ray, Apex's vice president, looked at Roger and appeared to reach out to shake hands. Roger angrily jumped up and said, "You son of a bitch," and hurriedly left the courtroom.

I stayed to get several copies of the memorandum signed by the parties, attorneys, and the judge. I told Apex's attorney I would have a draft of the Release in no later than two weeks.

When I returned to the office, it was about 5 p.m. and Roger had already left a message for me to call. I reached Roger and asked what he needed, and his response was simply could I come by his house about 7:30 tonight and explain the settlement to his wife. I told Roger I would be there along with my partner, Don, and Sanford Pomerantz. The three of us arrived at the home of Roger and Marie on time and went into the living room where Marie was seated with her cocktail. Also next to her were two beautiful whitish German Shepherds sitting with their eyes following our every move. They did not bark or move in any manner, but you felt their eyes on you as if protecting their masters.

As we sat down, Roger offered us cocktails or water, which we refused. I realized Roger had never told Marie about the settlement and this was not going to be an easy discussion. Marie, sitting in a large back chair with arms as if she were royalty, opened the conversation by inquiring as to the status of the trial. I responded by letting her know that we have spent the last three days in court attempting to settle this case. Marie started to fidget and looked straight at me and with fire in her eyes said, "We are not paying Apex one cent. Roger did nothing wrong." The two German Shepherds rose up and stood erect and were seemingly following the conversation.

I explained to Marie that we in fact reached a settlement and Roger had signed off on the resolution. I then had Sanford Pomerantz explain the benefits from the tax savings she and Roger would receive. I also reminded her of the possible criminal investigation by the IRS. I reminded Marie that by Roger testifying under oath, the IRS could use the testimony of Roger in the criminal case and Roger could go to prison.

Then came a response from Marie I will never forget. Angrily, Marie stood and said, "I don't give a fuck if he goes to jail. I am not going to pay those bastards one dollar." Without thinking, I lost my composure and yelled back, "You selfish bitch." "Roger," I said, "did you hear what she said?" As my voice rose, the two dogs growled and showed their teeth. That was all I needed to realize this was going nowhere. Roger had to restrain the dogs and pulled hard on their leashes and removed them from the room.

Sanford Pomerantz was freaking out and headed for the door. I turned my back on Marie and followed behind my partner, Don, and the three of us were out of the house and getting into Sanford Pomerantz's car. Roger came out just as we were backing out of this driveway. I got out of the car and told Roger he cannot back out of this settlement, as he signed the settlement memorandum with the basic terms. Apex could and would file suit to enforce settlement. As much as I wanted to make negative comments about Marie, I managed not to do so.

I told Roger he needed to concentrate all his efforts on getting as many Affidavits signed from the manufacturers as possible and as soon as possible. We had about 34 more days before I met with the IRS in Washington, D.C., to stop the criminal indictment.

As I left Roger's house, I could not help thinking that Roger may be better off in prison than living with Marie the rest of his life. I could not imagine living with someone who cared more about money than my well-being.

The hearing on my attorney's fees was scheduled in seven days, and I told Roger he could appear if he wanted, but it was not necessary. I would be the only witness to explain to the three judge panel all the work I had completed to justify my request for $100,000 in legal fees. The actual time spent on the trial and appeal was only about $20,000. Since I admitted Roger had committed commercial bribery for this matter only, there was no need for depositions or other discovery. The research was simple, as there had been no cases on ERISA prior to this one. I had relied on the wording of the law, as well as some scholarly article on ERISA which courts sometimes follow.

The simple issue was can a company take away an employee's pension once that employee is vested in the plan? I agreed and the U.S. Court of Appeals agreed with me that the company could not.

I testified that the issues in this case were unique and one of the first impression since there were no other cases interpreting ERISA to rely on. In addition, my client had run out of funds to pay me, and if I had not won, there was a good chance my client would never have been able to pay my fees. These were all factors for the Court to consider in allowing four or five times the actual fees.

After testifying for almost three hours, the panel adjourned and returned with its ruling after almost 40 minutes. The court ruled Apex must pay my attorney's fees in the sum of $35,000 up to this point. The Chief Judge on the panel reminded the attorney for Apex that if they appealed their decision to the Supreme Court of the United States and my client was again successful in getting his pension, the fees awarded would exceed $100,000. Naturally, any fees paid by Apex would be used to pay down Roger's balance of fees and costs. Apex had 30 days to appeal the court's ruling, and I was fairly certain Apex had enough with litigation. Some of the vendors sued in the other five states had paid money to Apex with no admission of wrongdoing. This was done to prevent large amounts of attorney's fees and the right to continue to do business with Apex. Only the vendor in Florida was prepared to fight the case and let a jury decide the case. Apex, as I thought, agreed to accept the Court's ruling on my attorney's fees.

Now the only case I had left for Roger was the IRS threat of criminal prosecution. Roger, I felt, could not emotionally or financially handle a full-fledged criminal trial with the possibility of prison time hanging over him. My plan was simply to try to convince the IRS that Roger had not performed any services for the cash gifts he had received and, therefore, the money was not taxable.

I met with Roger two weeks before my scheduled meeting with the IRS in Washington, D.C. Roger was successful in obtaining signed and notarized Affidavits from 27 manufacturers who each swore under oath that the cash gifts they gave to Roger each year were never deducted from their tax returns. The amounts mentioned in the Affidavits ranged from $1500 per year to $2500. The length of time these gifts were given ranged from 10 years to the most 32 years. In addition to these Affidavits, Roger was able to show by Affidavit of a spouse, child, or sibling that the person who made the gift to Roger was deceased. These totaled 14 Affidavits. Roger then provided me a list of names and last contact information for 19 other former vendors he received gifts from that he could not locate.

I was impressed with what a great job Roger had done to obtain all the signed Affidavits, and I told Roger he should not accompany me to the IRS meeting, but be close to his phone during the time of the meeting, as I may need to call him to answer possible questions.

I put all of the information Roger provided in a folder along with a biography of Roger showing his date of birth, education which stopped at high school, his employment history of 40 plus years with Apex, as well as the ruling on his pension by the U.S. Court of Appeals. I wanted the IRS agent to know something personal about Roger and not simply that he had a large amount of unreported cash in his safe deposit box. I made several copies of this folder to give to the IRS agent when we met.

I left St. Louis early Wednesday morning to fly to Reagan International Airport. With me was Sanford Pomerantz, the tax expert with whom I worked on this matter. Our meeting with the IRS was scheduled for 1 p.m. We arrived in Washington, D.C., at 11:45 and took a cab to the IRS office and arrived in plenty of time to get to the office of Agent Harold Glaser before 1 p.m.

As Sanford Pomerantz and I sat in the waiting room, I told him to be prepared to interrupt me if I state something that is incorrect regarding the tax regulations. I will only try to persuade the agent that the money Roger received was not in any manner taxable income and he had not tried to hide income from the IRS.

Slightly after 1 p.m., a man about 40 years of age with sleeves rolled up, collar unbuttoned, and tie slightly undone came into the waiting room and introduced himself as Harold Glaser. We followed him to a small back office about 8x10 feet with a metal desk and two folding chairs with no window. His college degrees were hanging on a wall behind him and some family photographs were on the metal desk. He had Roger's file on his desk, which was in a small folder with Roger's name on it along with a bunch of numbers.

We spent less than a couple of minutes with introductions, and I went immediately into my client's position on why the IRS should not proceed with criminal charges against Roger. I handed the folder I prepared to Harold and advised him there were additional copies available if he needed more to provide to his supervisors. I was aware Harold did not make the final decision on Roger's criminal matter for the IRS.

I started out by discussing Roger's age, his family, and his work history. I also went on say Roger had just completed a lengthy legal battle with Apex where he spent a lot of money, time, and energy not only fighting for his pension, but defending himself in five out of state cases and one Missouri case. This had taken place over almost three years, and my client was physically and mentally exhausted, having spent much of his retirement defending himself.

I referred to the money found in Roger's safe deposit box of which I knew the IRS was aware. I went on to state that this money was all gifts from numerous vendors Roger dealt with over 40 plus years as a buyer. No gift received exceeded over $3000 per year, and none of these gifts were deducted as an expense by the giver of these gifts. I told Harold to review the Affidavits in the folder which supported this position. I went on to point out those vendors who had died and those we could not locate. Certainly, we could not produce Affidavits from those two groups of vendors.

More importantly, I went on that there was no place in a tax return to report gifts received under $3000 per year. If Roger owes any taxes on these gifts, I continued, it would be a civil matter not a criminal matter. Roger owes no taxes on these gifts, as this was not earned income.

Harold responded by stating the fact that Roger had all that cash hidden in a safe deposit box, giving a strong indication of guilt and wrongdoing and an intentional act of deceiving the IRS and the United States. Harold said he would discuss this information with a committee and let Roger and I know their final decision in the next two weeks.

I became upset with Harold's response and I stood up looking down at Harold and with my voice much louder I said, "The IRS has the money and manpower to proceed with this criminal case, but my client does not. If you do proceed, I will defend Roger vigorously using these Affidavits. I expect to be successful in this defense, and I intend to go public with the IRS wrongfully abusing its power by filing criminal charges against a taxpayer who they know or should have known did not commit tax fraud."

As I was going through my tirade, Sanford Pomerantz was kicking me and pulling on my sport coat to try to get me to sit down and stop talking. Unfortunately, I could not stop and I went on for another five or so minutes. Harold just looked at me. When I finished and sat down, Harold asked if we had anything else to discuss. There was nothing else and the meeting ended just after 45 minutes.

Sanford Pomerantz and I left the IRS building and went to the airport for the flight home. It was not until we were on the plane flying home that Sanford Pomerantz turned to me and simply said it was not in the client's best interest to get so upset. The IRS has all the power, and to piss him off does not help anyone. Sanford Pomerantz said we cannot do anything more than wait to hear from the IRS but chances are they will start the criminal proceedings.

As I left Sanford Pomerantz and went home, I went over in my mind what I had said during my meeting with Harold, the IRS agent. The only thing I regretted was raising my voice and being emotional. However, I was passionate about the fact that my client was innocent of any criminal activity. I did not like the IRS threatening criminal action on this weak of a case. I would admit my client was stupid, at best, for hiding large amounts of cash in a safe deposit box. However, there is strong evidence that these cash payments were truly not taxable, as they were gifts. There was no evidence to date that these were payments for some benefit my client received. I believed I could successfully defend Roger in a criminal tax case. My anger came about because I knew such a case would break Roger financially and emotionally and that is not justice.

While I was awaiting word from the IRS, I cleared up loose ends on the Missouri case. The settlement documents were drafted and redrafted several times until both parties were satisfied with the wording. The payments agreed to were finally made to Apex by Roger. Roger received access to his safe deposit box and the remaining cash and stock certificates. One thing that Roger and I did not discuss as we were negotiating a settlement with Apex was that in finalizing the case for his pension, Roger received 34 months of pension benefits due plus interest. This was a substantial sum of money, but was not enough to lower the range of the anger Roger felt for Apex ownership. Some of that anger and bitterness spilled over to me, as he felt I had forced him to pay too much money to Apex to settle the commercial bribery case. It also did not help that he received my last bill for finalizing the commercial bribery case and my trip to Washington, D.C., to meet with the IRS, which also included Sanford Pomerantz's bill for fees and expenses. True to form, Roger tried to negotiate this bill, which I refused to do.

Now, the only matter left was to wait for the IRS' determination on criminal charges. It had been over two weeks since my face-to-face meeting with the IRS, and I was getting nervous. I had told Roger not to call, as I would call him immediately after I received the letter, plus he would also receive a copy of the determination letter.

The way the relationship with Roger had deteriorated, I was not sure Roger would retain me if criminal charges were brought by the IRS. By the same token, I was not sure I wanted to represent Roger who had not been completely truthful with me throughout the Apex case. In addition, Roger had expressed resentment over paying the legal fees.

Then almost 30 days from the time I met with Harold, the IRS agent, the letter I was expecting arrived with the official IRS envelope. I nervously opened the envelope and removed the letter. I unfolded the letter, which consisted of three paragraphs and signed by someone other than Harold Glaser, the agent I met with in Washington, D.C. The letter in part stated, "Upon review of additional information and upon further consideration, the Internal Revenue Service has made its final determination not to proceed against Roger for any criminal violation. This matter will be referred to the civil division of the IRS to determine if there are any taxes due."

Upon reading the letter over thoroughly several times, I was elated that Roger had escaped the ordeal of facing an exhausting and expensive criminal trial with the IRS.

I called my client at his home to make certain that he had received the good news. Marie answered the phone, and when I asked to talk to Roger, she very coldly replied that Roger was aware of the IRS decision, as he had received the same letter from the IRS. She went on to state that Roger no longer needed my services. Do not send another bill for legal services or costs, as it will not be paid. With that, she hung up.

That was my last conversation with Marie. Roger never called again. I wrote a last letter to Roger advising that I am closing my file, and he should call me to discuss any issues regarding any of the cases I handled for him regarding Apex.

As I looked back, I realized that a client may never truly appreciate the efforts and results of his attorney when the client views the facts of his case from a partial point of view. Roger always felt he was the victim who was harassed unfairly by Apex and taken advantage of by his attorney.

I never heard from Roger again. I can only surmise that Marie enjoyed the monthly pension benefits long after Roger's death.

CHAPTER II

⤛∞⤜

MARRIED IN DEATH

My receptionist advised me that a former client, Art Jackson, was on the phone and needed to talk to me about an urgent matter. I glanced at my watch and it was shortly before noon. I hesitated momentarily before picking up the receiver, as I could not recall Art Jackson or the subject matter in which I represented him.

Any potential new case is very important because my experience has taught me that you never know where a new case will lead. The new case could lead to more contacts for future business and the new case itself may have some substantial value.

As I started the conversation with Art, I tried to recall the matter in which I previously handled for him and whether or not I was successful. Unfortunately I could not recall my prior representation of Art Jackson.

As I listened to Art's story, I determined that he was African-American and had been satisfied with the results of my legal work on his behalf. Art then related the urgent matter to me.

Art had a cousin, Sharon Dawson, residing in Dyersburg, Tennessee, who was in her 70s. As a young girl, she married a young man who owned and operated a farm in Blytheville, Arkansas. The marriage took place in 1918. Shortly after the marriage, her husband, Jesse Dawson, went into the army in World War I and was sent to Europe where he stayed for over a year.

After the war, Jesse returned home to work on his farm, which consisted of over 200 acres. Art went on to state that his cousin Sharon only lived

47

with Jesse for just over 3 years and left him and never divorced. According to Art, Sharon had not seen Jesse for over 50 years. Jesse recently passed away and had left a large farm that had some value. Art wanted to know if his cousin Sharon could file some type of claim against Jesse's estate.

Art said he told his cousin that she should not use a local attorney in Blytheville or Dyersburg, which is just across the river from Blytheville, because he did not trust them since they all seem to know each other and worked closely together.

Art said he told Sharon he would drive her from Dyersburg to my office in St. Louis. Art told Sharon that I was the only attorney he knew who he would trust to handle this matter.

Art went on to state that his cousin did not have the money to pay attorney fees or expenses.

I told Art that I did not have enough facts to make a determination at this time, but I would be willing to meet with his cousin Sharon and if she does have a case I would handle it on a contingent fee basis. I told Art I would pay him for his time and expenses in driving to bring Sharon to my office and take her back home. We set a date for meeting with Sharon and our conversation ended.

As I now reflect on that initial conversation with Art, I wonder what forces were in place that a client such as Art would think enough of me to volunteer to drive from St. Louis to Dyersburg, Tennessee, and back to bring his cousin Sharon to meet with me and discuss her case that I may not be willing to take. Further, Art would need to make that trip again to take Sharon back home. I attribute this to some higher power that put Sharon and me together through her cousin Art.

The first meeting with Sharon Dawson was most interesting. Although an African-American, Sharon could pass for a Caucasian as she was an Albino. She was a little over 5 feet, thin, with grayish hair pulled back with a barrette.

Sharon had a positive attitude and was a delight to talk with. She brought her marriage license for me to review, which showed her date of marriage on March 12, 1918, to Jesse, in Blytheville, Arkansas.

I spent over two hours with her as she shared the details from the date of her marriage to Jesse until she arrived in my office.

Sharon's Story

Sharon met Jesse while she was visiting her family in Blytheville, which was just across the Mississippi River from Dyersburg. Sharon was a pretty young girl of 17 at the time and a little more than a year later Sharon and Jesse were married. Sharon was a happy young bride and life was good. Jesse's family had owned this very fertile farmland that they had been successful in operating.

Sharon and Jesse's life was interrupted when Jesse went into the army in WWI.

Jesse was sent to Europe and they were separated for almost two years before Jesse returned to Sharon.

In Sharon's mind, her life with Jesse would continue as before with Jesse being the successful farmer and Sharon at his side; however, it was not to be.

The army had changed Jesse and he had become more possessive and withdrawn.

Sharon said that one night she and Jesse went to a local hall where there was a neighborhood party with food and music. During the evening, a young man asked Sharon to dance and she accepted. According to Sharon, this was not out of the ordinary and she thought nothing of it. She was just having a good time.

Jesse, on the other hand, was quite upset. On the way home, Jesse confronted Sharon and told her that dancing with another man was unacceptable and there would be consequences.

Sharon, being pretty independent, was not one to be controlled and defiantly stared back at Jesse insisting she had done nothing wrong.

Before they went to bed that evening, Jesse became more argumentative and Sharon said she was not going to discuss this matter anymore.

Jesse left the room and came back seconds later with a handgun. He grabbed Sharon with one hand and pushed her down on the bed. Sharon tried to fight back, but to no avail. Jesse was too strong.

Suddenly a shot rang out and Sharon felt pain in her left thigh. Jesse had shot her. He then said, "If you ever dance with another man, the next time I will kill you."

SANFORD GOFFSTEIN

As Sharon said, back in the 1920s, the law just did not care about a black man shooting a black woman. This type of crime would usually go unreported.

It took about two months for the wound to heal enough for Sharon to be able to move about with only a slight limp.

Sharon then went on with her story. One morning, after she had fully recovered, she told Jesse she was going out into the fields to pick greens for dinner. Sharon put on as many layers of clothes as she could and went out the back door to the fields and never looked back. Sharon went north all the way to Chicago and far away from Blytheville and Jesse.

Sharon found work in Chicago making beds in a small hotel and general housekeeping. She was able to support herself and save some money. After several months, she went to see a lawyer about obtaining a divorce.

During the initial interview, the attorney asked for Jesse's full name and address along with other personal information about Jesse. When Sharon inquired why that information was necessary, the attorney advised her that he was required by law to serve the divorce petition and summons on Jesse. Jesse would have the option of coming to Chicago and contest the divorce.

After hearing this information, Sharon thanked the lawyer and ended the interview. Sharon was fearful that if Jesse knew where she was he would come to Chicago and carry out his threat to kill her. This was the only time Sharon ever thought of divorcing Jesse.

Sharon made a life for herself in Chicago, making new friends and attending church on a regular basis. After a few years in Chicago, Sharon met a nice man by the name of Harvey Miller. After dating for several months, Sharon and Harvey were married and she never told Harvey or anyone about her marriage to Jesse. Sharon was very happy being married to Harvey and lived a good life until Harvey died after a short illness in 1968. Having no children, Sharon decided to move back to Dyersburg, Tennessee, across the river from Jesse. At no time had Sharon seen or heard from Jesse since she left him in 1922.

Sharon first found out about Jesse's death from her cousin Art and he convinced Sharon to come with him to St. Louis to see if I would help her and determine whether she would be entitled to any distribution from Jesse's estate since she had never been divorced from Jesse as far as she knew.

At the time I interviewed Sharon, she had no information as to the value of Jesse's estate or the names of any heirs. Sharon was not sure whether or not, like her, Jesse had remarried or had any children. Sharon was sure she had received no divorce papers from Jesse.

After my interview with Sharon, I felt that the facts would show Sharon was still legally the wife of Jesse at the time of his death and she would be entitled to the statutory amount a wife could take by the law in Arkansas at the time of Jesse's death, provided that Jesse had not obtained a divorce by publication as opposed to personal service. There were no known heirs of Jesse.

I agreed to take this case on a contingent fee and I would advance all costs and expenses. There would be no fee nor would she have to reimburse my expenses if I did not recover any money for her. I told Sharon I would start on her case immediately and keep her advised as the case developed.

I thanked Art for driving Sharon back to Dyersburg and gave him all his expense money plus money for his time.

I had a good feeling about this case, but no real facts to support Sharon's claim except the marriage license Sharon brought with her.

After much thought, I made a decision to retain an attorney in Blytheville and pay him on an hourly basis and take all of the financial risks as opposed to splitting any potential fees. I was willing to take all the financial risks and be responsible for all costs including my local attorney's fees and expenses.

I was convinced that this was a special case and that for some unknown reason this case was meant for me. I believed Sharon and felt she was entitled to some reward from Jesse's estate.

The next day, I contacted an attorney in Blytheville whose name and background I found in Martindale-Hubbel (an international publication that rates lawyers by ability and ethics) by the name of Ron Hunter. Ron was in his early 50s with a general practice. He had no partners and one part-time associate.

I completed the financial arrangements with Ron and made a date to meet at his office. Ron said he would set a time to meet with the attorney for the estate, Alex Harris, who Ron knew.

It took over six hours to drive down to Blytheville. I had dinner that night with Ron and the next morning I met with Ron at his office at 9 a.m. The meeting with the attorney for Jesse's estate was not until 11 a.m.

Ron's office was filled with older furniture with two chairs in front of his desk and a working credenza behind. There were other files on the credenza where it appeared Ron does most of his work. The building, which housed Ron's office, was one story and had other commercial offices, but it appeared Ron was the only lawyer that was a tenant at that location.

Ron knew of Jesse's attorney for the estate, Alex Harris, who Ron described as an elderly attorney in his late sixties with an excellent reputation.

We arrived at Alex's office about five minutes early. He had a receptionist and a nicely decorated reception area. The receptionist escorted us into Alex Harris's office right on schedule and Alex, formally dressed with coat and tie, stood and directed us to a round table with five chairs next to a large window with a great view. Alex's office was quietly advertising, here is a very successful attorney.

After exchanging greetings and asking if his receptionist could get us anything to drink, we all seated ourselves around the table. I advised Alex that I had been retained to represent Sharon Dawson and her claim against the estate of Jesse Dawson as his wife. I showed Alex a copy of the marriage license of Sharon and Jesse with their signatures as well as the signature of the Justice of the Peace. I told Alex he could keep this copy for his file.

The reaction I received from Alex caught me by surprise. Alex took the copy of the marriage license and just smiled. Alex went on to state that he had known Jesse Dawson all his life and was positive Jesse had never married. He went on to state that Jesse's only living heirs were his cousins, all of whom resided in southern California.

Alex rejected outright the fact that Sharon claimed to be Jesse's widow. He said the marriage license proved nothing as far as he was concerned and Alex let me know he would vigorously defend any claim Sharon would make against the estate.

As Ron and I left Alex's office, I became concerned that I had made a mistake by taking responsibility for all legal fees and expenses as this matter could turn into lengthy litigation, which could be quite expensive, and there was no guarantee of a successful outcome.

Alex did provide us with an inventory of Jesse's estate, which included approximately 240 acres of farmland that had an unknown value and approximately $350,000 of cash and marketable securities.

As we got into Ron's car, he suggested we stop by the Recorder of Deeds office, which was only about ten minutes away. I looked at Ron with a puzzling look as I did not have a clue as to why we should make a trip to the Recorder of Deeds office in Blytheville. I inquired of Ron of what would be so important that we should stop at the Recorder of Deeds.

Ron patiently responded by explaining simply that it was a known fact that many World War I veterans recorded their discharge papers as Congress in the days after the war was providing benefits for World War I veterans and many of the veterans were recording their discharge papers to have proof that they served in World War I in case they lost their discharge papers.

This was a revelation to me and something I would never have thought of on my own. How fortunate I was to have retained Ron.

As we went to the office of the Recorder of Deeds, we went to the Record Center and talked with a young clerk. Ron told her that we were looking for discharge papers of an individual and the clerk directed us to a cabinet where we could locate documents filed by any individual. The documents were listed in alphabetical order. This was before computers.

We then went through the index and spent a little more than an hour and then we found the document we were looking for and the location where it was stored. We gave the information to the clerk and shortly she brought the discharge papers of Jesse Dawson that had been recorded shortly after his discharge from the army. As Ron and I went through Jesse's discharge papers, we found what we were looking for: Jesse's serial number, which was like the lost key to a treasure box. This number could open a lot of doors to successfully litigating or settling this case.

Ron already had earned his fee with his suggestion of visiting the Recorder's office. I would have never thought about this idea.

Another bit of fortune was that the Recorder Center for all military records was located in St. Louis County just 10 miles from my office.

When we returned to Ron's office, I called my partner, Rod Weiss, gave him Jesse's serial number and told him to immediately go to the Record Center and look up Jesse's file and if necessary get copies of Jesse

Dawson's military records, specifically any records showing payments made to his wife, Sharon.

I told Rod to call me immediately after he reviewed Jesse's military records and let me know what information he obtained.

Rod Weiss was my first partner and a very bright individual. He was my first mentor in how to practice law and together we started the law firm of Weiss & Goffstein.

Rod, true to his word, immediately left the office and drove to the Record Center on Page Avenue. It was almost two hours later when Rod called me at Ron's office. This was before the general public thought about cell phones.

Rod explained that the records of Jesse Dawson were available for inspection and he found the key documents that I needed to prove that Sharon was the wife of Jesse Dawson. In the military records of Jesse Dawson were the records for allotment payments to Sharon. This form signed by Jesse authorized a monthly sum of money to be paid to Sharon from Jesse's monthly pay. In addition, Sharon was designated as the beneficiary on the life insurance policy Jesse had obtained from the army.

Once again, it seemed to me that some higher power had intervened to provide my client with key evidence to support her claim against the estate of her husband whom she had not seen in almost 50 years.

Armed with this additional evidence, which strongly supported my client's claim, I made another appointment to meet with Alex, the attorney for Jesse's estate. I had in my briefcase a certified copy of the allotment documents Jesse Dawson had completed over 50 years ago authorizing the U.S. Army to send a monthly check to my client, Sharon Dawson, who was shown as the wife of Jesse Dawson. Thanks to my local counsel, Ron Hunter, we had the evidence to go forward, if necessary, with a claim against the estate.

Ron had also completed his research of the Arkansas law which indicated that since Jesse had no children, there was a good possibility a surviving spouse would be entitled to 100 percent of the estate and the only surviving relatives, the first cousins residing in California, would receive nothing.

At the beginning of the meeting, Alex was very cordial and inquired as to what documents we were bringing to him to review since he was positive his client, Jesse Dawson, had never married.

I handed Alex the certified copy of the allotment documents and he took his time reviewing all three pages. The documents had Jesse's serial number, his social security number, and his signature, which Alex recognized. The documents also showed Sharon as the recipient of these payments.

Together with the marriage license, the allotment documents convinced Alex that my client was the wife of Jesse and she had a lawful claim, but for no more than fifty percent of the estate if that much. I had Ron, my local counsel, explain to Alex the probate law in effect that could give Sharon the entire estate.

Alex said that he would defend the claim of Sharon for 100 percent of the estate but would be willing to discuss a claim in the range of 40 to 50 percent of the estate.

I called Sharon and discussed the options she had. I explained to her why my local counsel felt she could possibly receive the entire estate. I told Sharon that to get the entire estate she would be facing almost two years of litigation and more with appeals. There was also a question of the value of the farmland.

I left Alex's office with the understanding that I would meet with my client and get back to him with a firm settlement proposal.

My old client Art brought Sharon back to St. Louis and we discussed her options. Sharon was not interested in lengthy litigation because she was 78 years old and she would like to enjoy the benefits of her settlement. Sharon also felt Jesse's cousins were entitled to share in the estate and as she said, "after all, I had not seen Jesse in over 50 years." I suggested to Sharon that we claim all of the liquid assets, worth close to $350,000, and she give up her claim against the farmland, which had an unknown value, leaving that asset to the cousins.

Jesse was to receive close to $200,000 after my contingent fee. This was more money than she ever had at any time in her life.

I then contacted the estate attorney, Alex Harris, and finalized a settlement giving Sharon all the liquid assets. This settlement was approved by the Probate Court of Blytheville, Arkansas.

Within 15 days of the approval, I received a $347,918 check from Jesse's estate. After I took my contingent fee, I put the remainder in three separate bank accounts in trust with myself as trustee for the benefit of Sharon Dawson. Sharon and I had discussed if she had put her money in a bank in Dyersburg, Tennessee, the whole city would know in short time. Sharon wanted no one in Dyersburg to know of this money.

Sharon agreed that I would give her $10,000 initially and send her money, as she needed it in $10,000 increments. Although this $10,000 amount would raise some eyebrows in Dyersburg, it would not be as great if Sharon had deposited over $150,000.

From my fee, I paid Ron Hunter his bill plus a $2500 bonus for his excellent work as my local counsel.

I met with Art Jackson, who had worked so hard to bring Sharon from Dyersburg, Tennessee, to my office. I thanked Art for all that he had done to get this case to me and I paid him for his time and expenses. Since it was also close to his birthday, I gave Art a nice check for his birthday.

As I look back on this case, I believe that fate intervened in some manner that had Art pick me as Sharon's attorney. I had fortunately picked an excellent attorney in Blytheville, Arkansas, who suggested checking the Recorder of Deeds office, and that Jesse did in fact record his discharge papers. The fact that the Record Center was only miles from my office to find Jesse's military records was a bonus. The allotment records my partner found sealed the deal. Whether it was fate, luck, or a higher power, I was truly grateful.

CHAPTER III

THE DEFECTIVE TRACTOR

I received the call on a late Friday afternoon when I was straightening the files on my desk, ready to get an early start for the weekend.

My receptionist said that I had a call from Harold Simmons from Seattle, Washington, who had been referred to me by my good friend and long-time client Marv Sherman.

I thought before I even picked up the phone that if Marv had referred this client, then there must be some substance to whatever Mr. Simmons wanted to discuss.

I picked up the phone and, after exchanging pleasantries, Harold advised me that he is currently working as an auditor with the Department of Insurance for the state of Washington. He had met Marv when he held a similar position with the state of Missouri.

Marv Sherman was the president and owner of an extremely successful insurance agency. His agency was the Managing General Agent for an insurance carrier and Harold had on occasion been one of the auditors who would examine and audit the claims files being handled by Marv's claims department.

Harold said he had a case that he wanted to refer to me and Marv told Harold that I was the attorney he should use.

Harold spent the next thirty minutes providing me with the background and his involvement with the person he wished to refer to me. Harold, a single person, had traveled to Miami Beach for a week's vacation. One evening he went to a local bar and, as was his intent, met a woman with whom he shared a few drinks. As the night went on, they became more intimate and Harold was invited to spend the night at this woman's home. Harold stayed all night and in the morning he had breakfast with his new friend, Betty, and her son, Jeff. Harold described Jeff as a nice-looking 15-year-old, 5 feet 10 inches tall. Noticeably, Jeff was missing half of his right hand, part of his right arm, and the right leg just below the knee. According to Harold, Jeff's right hand looked like the claw of a lobster. After getting over the initial shock, Harold asked Betty to tell him how Jeff had received these injuries. Betty went on to tell Harold the following story.

Betty had been living in Caliber, Iowa, since before Jeff was born, which is where she currently resided. One day, when Jeff was about 18 months old, she took Jeff to visit her cousin Alice on a farm just outside of Caliber. At the time, Alice was living with a local priest who owned the farm. Betty and Alice decided to go shopping in town and Betty left Jeff with the priest's housekeeper.

It was a beautiful, warm summer day and the housekeeper spread a large blanket outside on the backyard grass. The blanket was laid out about 20 feet from the kitchen door and the housekeeper was able to keep an eye on Jeff while she was preparing a meal for the priest and his guests.

At about this time, a young parishioner by the name of Rick came by the house to cut the grass for the priest as he had volunteered to do. The yard was about 1/2 acre and the priest owned a small tractor that Rick could use to cut the grass. Rick had used this riding tractor several times before without any problems.

On this day, Rick started cutting the back of the yard first and worked his way toward the house. Rick was aware that Jeff was alone on the blanket just playing with the little toys set out by the housekeeper. As Rick came within 10 to 15 feet of the young child, Rick took steps to make certain that Jeff was safe.

Rick stopped the tractor and put the gear in neutral. Rick left the motor running. As Rick took several steps toward the blanket with the intent to move Jeff and the blanket, the tractor suddenly jumped into gear and ran over Rick's right shoe and then went slightly to the right and ran over Jeff lying on the blanket. Rick was horrified as he saw the young child lying on the blanket, bloody with his little body in several pieces. Rick had attempted to stop the runaway tractor, to no avail.

The housekeeper, screaming, ran out and grabbed the baby and wrapped all the pieces that had been cut from Jeff's body and sought medical help.

Now Harold was looking at Jeff almost 14 years after this horrific incident, missing part of his right leg and his claw-like right hand. Jeff wore a prosthesis on his right leg. Harold described Jeff as a likeable kid with a good attitude.

Harold inquired as to whether Betty had retained an attorney to seek damages for the disabling injuries to Jeff. Betty said she had two previous attorneys, but each one was unable to be successful. It seems that the priest left Iowa with Alice and went west to California. Neither attorney had been successful in finding some individual or entity to sue in order to compensate Jeff for his injuries. Betty said she just had given up and felt that she and her son would simply have to accept this situation, as bad as it was, and learn to live with it.

Harold convinced Betty to let him find an attorney to represent Jeff. As a result, Harold called my friend Marv in St. Louis and, after getting my name and number, called me.

Harold gave me Betty's phone number and said he would call Betty and tell her I would be calling her.

After I hung up the phone, I reflected on the information just given to me by Harold. First this was a case that had a lot of monetary value due to the seriousness of the injuries. The mother lost any claim she may have because of the statute of limitations. Since Jeff was still a minor, he had a claim until 21 years old plus the statute of limitations in Iowa. At the time, I did not know how many years that would be. The negative in taking the case was whom would I sue. My choices were the parishioner who was volunteering his services and probably had no or minimal insurance coverage; the priest, who is no longer around and may have had no insurance coverage; the church itself might be a possibility; lastly, the manufacturer of the tractor if I could prove a defect in the design of the tractor. In order to find a defect, I needed to know the model of the tractor the parishioner used that day when the tragedy occurred. Hopefully the tractor that was used was still on the premises and could be identified as the tractor that was used and caused the injuries to Jeff. I had enough information from Harold's call that led me to the decision to take the case.

I knew the injuries were so horrific the target defendant would not want to risk a trial. The statute of limitations would not be a problem because Jeff was only 15 and I would have a lot of time to file suit. My target defendant had to be the manufacturer, as they would have the ability to pay any judgment. I would definitely need the make and model number of the tractor. This would be a difficult case and I would probably have to bring suit in Iowa and retain a local attorney. This was a real crapshoot, but the injuries made it worthwhile.

After making the decision to take this case, I called Betty and advised her that I would represent Jeff on a contingent fee basis and I would advance all costs and try and get compensation for her son's injuries. I told Betty this would be a difficult case against the manufacturer and reminded her that if we received any money it would have to go in a trust for the benefit of Jeff and that none of the money would go to her. Betty and I made plans to meet at a restaurant close to the dealer where the tractor was originally purchased. Betty seemed happy that I was willing to take on her son's case. The meeting was set for the following week.

In order to get to Caliber, Iowa, I had to fly to Des Moines, rent a car, then drive for about one and one-half hours. I arrived at about 9:30 p.m. and checked into a motel. I got a good night's sleep and was up early and prepared to meet my clients at 9 a.m. at a local restaurant less than two blocks from the dealer's store.

I arrived at the restaurant about ten minutes early and saw a woman in her mid to late forties standing outside next to a young man who was about 6'2" tall and had his one hand in his coat pocket. I guessed correctly that this was my client, Jeff, with his mother, Betty. We exchanged greetings and then went inside the restaurant to start my initial conference with my new client.

I explained to Betty that any claim she might have had for the injuries sustained by Jeff were barred by the 5-year statute of limitations in Missouri and may be less in Iowa where the injuries occurred.

I advised Betty that Jeff's claim was still viable since he was a minor and the statute of limitations did not start to run on his claim until he reached 21 years of age.

I had Betty sign my employment contract as Jeff's natural guardian and assured her that she was not obligated to pay me any money for my services nor for any expenses incurred. My fees and expenses would be paid from any moneys I received either by settlement or suit.

We then went over Betty's version as to how this terrible accident happened to Jeff. Betty identified all of the people with knowledge of this tragedy.

The most important information I received from Betty in our initial meeting was that she had met with the tractor dealer and he informed Betty that he had all the records from the sale of the tractor to the local priest. This was significant as this would help me identify the make and model number of the tractor from which I would request the blueprints from the manufacturer to assist me in proving the tractor was defective in its design which caused the tractor to jump into gear from neutral while running.

When we finished our meeting the three of us went to the dealer to get copies of the records he had on the sale of the tractor.

As we approached the store, you could see the famous manufacturer's bright colored logo hanging over the front door. As we opened the front door, I noticed the gentleman behind the counter look up and had a somewhat disgusted look. Fortunately we were the only people in the store at 11 a.m. that morning. Betty said good morning and introduced me to George, the owner. I told George that Betty had been retained me as the attorney for Jeff. I asked George if I could review all the documents he had on the sale of the riding tractor to the local priest more than 15 years ago. I told George that I would want to make a complete copy of this file.

George appeared nervous and somewhat angry in his response. Much to the surprise of my client and his mother, George responded by saying he had no records of the sale of the tractor to the priest. George went on to state that he routinely destroys all his records after ten years. I reminded George that just three weeks earlier he had told Betty he had these records and I find it hard to believe that the records are no longer available. I am fairly certain George was aware of the injuries sustained by Jeff and how the accident occurred.

George, now in a raised voice, again denied having these records and said Betty was mistaken as to what she thought she previously heard.

Betty was extremely upset with George's comments and knew he was not being truthful and was intentionally withholding key information from us.

I told Betty that without these documents I would never be able to pursue a case against the manufacturer. There would be no way I could prove the tractor was defective in its design without the model and serial number. When I left Betty and Jeff to start my trip back home, the three of us were very disappointed. I told them that there was no way I could be successful in a suit against the manufacturer without the blueprints of the tractor, as any expert I would retain would need to study these key documents in order to prove a case of defective design against the manufacturer.

I drove back to Des Moines and caught the first flight back to St. Louis. During the trip home, I thought that maybe it just wasn't meant to be. Too much time had passed and there was no evidence available to help Jeff receive compensation for the horrific injuries he sustained through no fault of his own.

I had little hope of coming up with a solution to help Jeff receive some financial award for all the damages and suffering he had gone through and would go through for the next sixty years of his life. I felt my chance of a successful recovery for Jeff was less than 10 percent.

I returned to the office and concentrated on other matters that needed my immediate attention. Jeff, Betty, and the tractor were put on the back burner for the moment. One of these matters was pending in the county of St. Charles where the courthouse in the city of St. Charles was a mere 25 minutes from my office. I had probably been to the St. Charles Courthouse hundreds of times in my career prior to this day. I was appearing for a case management conference. As I was going west on Highway 70 just about 10 minutes from the St. Charles Courthouse, I noticed for the first time the manufacturer's bright colored sign advertising a dealership located in St. Charles County.

I am quite certain that I had driven past that same sign for years without noticing it, but this day the sign stood out like the brightest fireworks display on the Fourth of July.

My mind started racing and I began to formulate a plan on how to proceed in helping Jeff and his mother. It was still a long shot, but my odds at success for Jeff jumped from under 10 percent to 50 percent.

The case management conference took a back seat to Jeff's case as I hurried through the conference to get back to my office. Once back in my office, I met with my partner and put the plan into action. First I filed suit against the manufacturer in St. Charles County where they were doing business through that dealership whose sign was the impetus for my plan. The owner of the local dealership was served with a petition and summons. As expected, the attorneys for the manufacturer filed a Motion to Dismiss the suit arguing that the correct jurisdiction was where the accident occurred, which would have been Iowa, not St. Charles, Missouri. I had anticipated this motion and, fortunately for my client and me, the current law at that time favored the case being tried in St. Charles County and the Court overruled the Motion to Dismiss.

The second step in my plan was to issue subpoenas to the dealer in Iowa and to the young man who was driving the riding tractor that had run over Jeff many years earlier. The subpoena to George, the dealer in Caliber, Iowa, was a *subpoena duces tecum* that required him to produce all documents in his possession that relate to the riding tractor he sold to the priest. I was hoping that I was correct that George had been lying when he said he had destroyed these records. It was a gamble but one worth taking.

The second subpoena was to Rick, the driver of the tractor, so I could question him in detail about the events that occurred more than 15 years ago, leaving Jeff with loss of one limb and part of his hand.

The depositions were both set on the same day in Caliber two hours apart in a conference room in the hotel where I was staying.

For a second time, I flew to Des Moines, rented a car at the airport, and drove to Caliber. During the entire time I was traveling, I felt upbeat about the chance that the dealer had been lying and he would come to the deposition with all the documents requested in the subpoena. I had not received a call from George or an attorney representing him that said there were no documents responsive to the subpoena in his possession.

I did receive a call from Rick several days before the deposition. Rick said he was relieved that he could finally tell his side of the story of what had occurred that day. Rick said he had been living with guilt ever since the accident over 15 years ago and he was eager to testify as to what actually happened that unforgettable day.

I advised Rick that he would be questioned at length by the attorney retained by the manufacturer who would try to prove that the terrible incident and the damages to Jeff were all the fault of Rick and not caused by any malfunction of the tractor. I told Rick I could not represent him but that I was trying to prove that the injuries to Jeff happened all as a result of the defective design of the tractor. I suggested to Rick that he may want to retain a lawyer for this deposition who could make objections to questions put to Rick by both attorneys. Rick said he would think about it but would probably come alone.

The depositions were scheduled for Tuesday morning at 10 a.m. The night before the deposition, I reviewed the few notes I had and tried to get a good night's rest. Unfortunately I couldn't sleep as I kept thinking what if my intuition was wrong and George did not have any records. I kept thinking that George could have destroyed the records as he claimed when I first met him or after I first met him. I tossed and turned all night.

Finally the alarm went off at 7 a.m. I showered, dressed, and went for a light breakfast in the hotel dining room. Once again I reviewed my notes and I was ready to proceed with the depositions.

I met my clients in the hotel lobby and advised them that I would start with George before deposing Rick. I told them they could take notes but not to make any comments or show any emotion as the testimony unfolded.

When we arrived at the conference room, it was 9:30 and both George and Rick were present. The court reporter had not yet arrived nor had the manufacturer's attorney, Phil Morrisey.

To my delight, I noticed that George held onto a small briefcase and he would not look at me but looked down toward the floor and he appeared nervous. I introduced myself to Rick, who was a nice-looking man in his forties. He had a firm handshake but slightly wet from perspiration. I reintroduced myself to George and extended my hand, which he ignored. I then asked him if he brought the documents that I had subpoenaed, and he nodded affirmatively.

About 9:45 the Court Reporter appeared with her machinery and after introductions she started to set up her equipment.

About five minutes later, Phil showed up with his large briefcase, alone, and no representative of the manufacturer was with him. Phil's main objective was to protect his client and its insurer. One of his best arguments was that the injuries to Jeff were solely caused by Rick's negligence in operating the riding tractor and not by any defect in the tractor. Phil was a seasoned defense attorney and I was sure he would do a great job on cross-examination of Rick and go into great detail of every movement Rick made in the operation of the tractor from the first turn of the ignition switch to the stopping of the tractor after it had run over the little baby, Jeff, lying helplessly on the blanket just outside the kitchen door that unforgettable day.

The deposition started promptly at 10 a.m. and George was sworn in by the Court Reporter. After outlining the standard rules of depositions to the witness, I asked George if he had reviewed the *subpoena duces tecum* to produce documents that had been served upon him several weeks ago and George admitted that he had. I then asked if he had an attorney to represent him, to which he replied "no." I then asked if there was anything he did not understand about the subpoena he had read and again he answered "no."

I proceeded to ask George if he had brought with him documents that were responsive to the subpoena and he said he had. At this time, my heart began to beat a little faster and nervously, as I asked him to put all of the documents on the table so I may review them, which he did.

To my delight, I saw the invoice, the delivery ticket, a warranty, and manual on the tractor, which had the make and model number. This was similar to finding a lottery ticket that hopefully had the winning numbers. Now I had all the information necessary to provide to my expert, Boulter Kelsey, who would be the one to determine whether I could make a case for a jury to determine the negligence of the manufacturer in its design. After making sufficient copies of each of the documents produced by George, the last question I asked was why he lied when he told my clients and me he no longer had these documents. Interestingly he responded by saying when he lied to me he wasn't under oath, but today he was obligated to tell the truth. I had questioned George for about forty minutes and Phil had no questions. It was apparent to me that Phil had already talked to George and had received copies of these documents before the deposition. I felt pretty certain that after receiving the subpoena, George had contacted the manufacturer and they put Phil in touch with George.

After a 15-minute break, it was Rick's turn. I knew this would take hours and I wasn't wrong. We went straight through without lunch, taking a break every ninety minutes or so. The deposition did not end until almost 6 p.m.

I started the questioning and as the deposition went on it seemed that Rick was unloading a heavy burden he had carried for years and was extremely happy to rid himself of this burden.

Rick said he was a member of the priest's church as had been his parents. He often volunteered to mow the land at the priest's home and would do so without making a prearranged time. The tractor in question was less than a year old and Rick had used this tractor approximately 12 times before this terrible incident. Rick had never had any problems in the operation of this tractor. Rick described the area that he mowed as mostly level but some areas sloped slightly. It normally took Rick about two hours to mow this area.

On the day in question, Rick recalled it was a warm, sunny day and he arrived just before 1 p.m. He saw the baby Jeff playing on the blanket. He told the housekeeper he was going to mow the land and he was given a cold glass of water. Rick proceeded to pull the cord and the tractor started up immediately, as it usually did. Rick started cutting in the back land going back and forth, cutting in rows. At least a couple of times Rick would stop the tractor, put it in neutral, and remove a large rock or piece of fallen tree that was in his way. Rick would never turn the motor off because he would have to start all over by pulling the cord to get the motor started and this was quite frankly a pain in the ass.

Rick went on to state that as he was in the last stages of cutting the acreage, as usual he finished by cutting the area close to the house. Rick saw Jeff just lying quietly on the blanket. The tractor was about 15 feet from the blanket and Rick waved to the housekeeper who was looking out the kitchen window.

I then asked Rick to explain what happened from that point on as accurately as possible. Rick's demeanor changed and I noticed tears welling in his eyes. Rick told the following: I got off the tractor after putting the gear in neutral as I have always done. I took about eight steps toward the baby to move him to a safe place when suddenly he felt the tractor run over his right shoe from the heel to the toe on the right side. He fell to the left and regained his balance to try and protect Jeff, but it was too late. The tractor went right in Jeff's direction and ran over the left side of Jeff. Rick was able to stop the tractor, but too late. He heard the housekeeper scream and the back door slam shut as the housekeeper ran down the steps to Jeff.

When Rick turned around, the housekeeper was holding the baby and the baby's severed parts were on the ground. She yelled for Rick to go into the house, grab a blanket and they would drive to the hospital with Jeff and the parts that were severed.

As Rick completed his testimony in response to my questions, he was sobbing and we took a recess for Rick to take time to compose himself, which was difficult. At that time, we recessed for about 20 minutes.

The cross-examination by the manufacturer's attorney started and Rick had recovered somewhat but was still nervous. The cross-exam centered on Rick's memory concerning his putting the tractor in gear when he stopped the tractor to move Jeff. Rick was asked to describe in detail the different gears on the tractor. Rick responded accurately. Then Rick was asked to describe the distance between neutral gear and the forward gear and Rick had no recollection other than a guess of an inch or less. Then Phil asked Rick whether it was possible that he had moved the gear from forward and intended to move to neutral but had not completed the shift to neutral. Rick said he believed he had put the gear firmly in neutral.

Phil followed up with whether or not it was remotely possible the gear was not firmly placed in neutral and Rick hesitated for what seemed like a minute as I nervously held my breath and responded with certainty that he was positive the gear was firmly placed in neutral when he went to move Jeff.

Phil then asked Rick to explain why the tractor would suddenly move forward if the gear was in neutral. Jeff responded that he had no idea and I objected that this called for an expert opinion.

Rick was questioned about the slope of the ground, if any, at the point where he stopped the tractor. I must admit I had not thought of that being an issue as I was more focused on Jeff's serious injuries. As I heard Rick testify as to the topography of that real estate, my heart started beating a little faster. Rick's description was that there was a gentle slope downward toward where Jeff was lying. Jeff could only guess the slope was about 10 degrees, but that was only a guess.

Phil then asked Rick if he thought it possible that even if the gear had been put in neutral that with the motor running the vibration could have caused the tractor to roll down the slope and run over Jeff. I immediately objected as calling for conjecture and speculation. Rick looked a little bewildered and hesitantly said with his head looking down at the table that he just didn't know if that were possible.

I noticed tears welling up in Rick's eyes once again and I realized looking at Rick's body language he felt that maybe this is what had happened. Although I knew that the manufacturer could not prove this possibility without an expert, the average juror could reach this conclusion.

Phil ended his questioning at about 5:45 p.m. I decided not to ask any more questions of Rick as I felt he had gone through enough, having to relive that terrible day and reliving the serious injuries that Jeff sustained.

I concluded after those two depositions that the defense would be that Rick had not put the gear in neutral, but just thought he did and the vibration of the tractor and the slope of the ground caused the tractor to run over poor Jeff through no fault on the part of the manufacturer. They would blame everything on Rick and had sufficient facts to do so.

I was in desperate need of the blueprints for the tractor to get to my expert, Boulter Kelsey, to see what information he could provide to get my case to a jury.

I told my clients, Betty and Jeff, the depositions went well and our chances of receiving money either by settlement or a jury verdict had just increased from zero to fifty percent.

I couldn't wait to get back to St. Louis and set up a meeting with Boulter and retain him as my expert in this case as his opinion would be the key to success. I knew that my costs for an expert could reach $25,000 through trial and about $10,000 for an opinion. I had used Boulter on three previous cases, all which resulted in favorable results.

I had placed a call for Boulter and as busy as he was since he was in demand by both attorneys for the injured as well as defense attorney, he returned my call the same day. We arranged a meeting at his office two days later. His office was a small house which had been converted into a couple of offices and a laboratory with all kinds of instruments for conducting tests on any product he was retained to give an opinion. (Once on a case I had retained him, he purchased the front chassis of a '94 vehicle to test whether the sudden lock-up of brakes on a car going 75 miles per hour was caused by an admittedly bad brake repair my client's employee had completed just two days before and caused serious injury to the young 17-year-old driver.)

At the initial meeting with Boulter, I showed him the documents I had received from the dealer. He advised me of the documents I needed to request from the manufacturer in order to have enough information to determine whether the tractor in question had a design defect. He also provided me with a list of questions to add to my standard interrogatories.

The key according to Boulter was to obtain all the plans, drawings, and any changes from the originals that describe in detail all the parts used in the manufacture of this tractor. Boulter wanted all this information from the date the tractor was originally designed to the date of purchase.

In the initial meeting, Boulter told me he was aware of a device that could have been installed directly under the seat of the tractor that was sensitive to the weight of the driver. The purpose of this device, according to my expert, was to automatically turn off the motor when the driver stood up from the seat to step off the tractor. This made the tractor much safer, but the manufacturers, for the most part, refused to install this safety device because it was too inconvenient for the driver as they would have to take the additional time to restart the tractor. This device, which he referred to as the "automatic shut-off" part, could have been installed at a cost of no more than 75 cents per device. Boulter was saying in effect that the manufacturer was willing to risk the safety for someone like my client for the convenience of the driver and more sales of this unsafe product for the manufacturer.

I thought this would be a good theme for my closing argument in the event I couldn't settle this case and it had to be tried to a jury.

Using my notes from my initial meeting with my expert, I prepared interrogatories that are questions to the manufacturer to answer under oath and prepared Request for Production of Documents asking for the documents needed by my expert to form an opinion as to the defect in the design of this particular tractor.

As expected, the manufacturer initially objected to producing any of the documents as to the design of the tractor, as it was proprietary and could not be published. I agreed to a very restricted Protective Order prepared by the manufacturer's attorney that limited these documents to any attorney in my office working on this case and of course my expert. This was all I needed to make my case.

As soon as I received the documents from the attorney for the manufacturer, I immediately delivered them to Boulter and received his promise that he would have an answer for me in less than two weeks. I called my clients and informed them as to the status of their case and that I now thought the chance of recovery to be about 75 percent. I reminded Betty that any moneys recovered for Jeff after fees and costs would be strictly for Jeff and would have to be put in probate until Jeff reached 21 years of age. Any monies that were taken from this minor's probate estate would have to be done by an order from the Court. Also the Probate Court would have to appoint a guardian for Jeff's estate and the estate would have to be opened initially in St. Charles to receive any monies from the settlement and then transferred to an estate to be opened up in their city. Betty said she was okay with this, but I was having doubts as this was about the fourth time Betty asked as to how much she would receive from any settlement.

True to his word, my expert called ten days after I had delivered the documents and told me that, just as he had suspected, the drawings he reviewed regarding the manufacture of this particular riding tractor did not provide for the automatic shut-off device. Boulter said that he could testify with absolute certainty that this device could have been added to the tractor at a cost of less than 75 cents per unit. He said that adding this device, although safer, would probably affect the sales of this product due to the inconvenience of having to restart the tractor each time the operator got up off the seat, which would cause it to automatically shut off.

This device certainly would have prevented the injuries to my client.

I knew at that moment the difficulty the manufacturer's attorney would have trying to argue that convenience in operating the tractor was more important than the safety to unprotected individuals such as Jeff. I now felt that there was a 90 percent chance that at some point before trial the manufacturer would try and resolve this case.

Boulter then asked if he could find a similar tractor that ran over Jeff and run several tests to see if he could duplicate the tractor jumping from neutral into forward gear as described by the driver, Rick, in his deposition. He said it would be difficult finding a duplicate of the actual tractor since it is no longer being manufactured. The last time this tractor was manufactured was about eight years earlier.

Boulter also opined that if he could get the tractor to jump from neutral into forward gear while idling, it would make the case stronger against the manufacturer. He estimated that the cost of an old tractor would be around $700 and his additional fees for testing would be another $5000. I felt this would be a good investment, and I authorized this expense.

The important fact to know when handling cases on a contingent fee basis is that you never want to be second best. Losing a case handled on a contingent fee can be quite expensive as not only do you spend hours without income, you can't work on income-producing cases while working on the contingent fee case. Also you advance monies for costs of depositions, court costs, and experts' fees. This is why you charge a 40 percent fee on contingent cases and sometimes as much as 50 percent if the case is appealed. Losing a contingent fee case could sometimes be like losing income for 6 to 9 months.

During the discovery phase of this litigation, I provided the manufacturer's attorney with a list of all past medical expenses and future projected medical expenses that, among other items, included a new prosthesis every three years. In addition I retained an economist who provided a figure for Jeff's future economic loss due to his physical limitations. I projected past and future medical to be in the $300,000 range and future economic loss in the $500,000 range. I knew that the manufacturer would retain experts that would contest the future medical and economic loss figures.

At the case management conference, I was able to procure a trial date three months in the future for a weeklong jury trial.

I told the attorney for the manufacturer my expert's theory on the defective design of the tractor and provided him with photos of my client's current condition that were with and without the prosthesis. These pictures alone were worth a thousand words, as the saying goes, but in this case worth hundreds of thousands of dollars without regards to the manufacturer's liability for defective design. I knew that at some point in the near future there would be settlement discussions. The problem I would have is whether the client would be willing to refuse the first several offers as I expected they would be more money than Betty had ever seen. I was concerned she would be unwilling to reject a first offer of what I imagined would be in the $500,000 range and risk going to trial. Since you can never guarantee what a jury will do, every offer rejected is similar to gambling. By rejecting an offer, you are betting you will receive a larger sum of money from a jury.

A good lawyer will know when the risk is too great to gamble and will know when the other side says "this is my final offer" that this is as big a falsehood as "the check is in the mail."

My second issue was to make sure Betty understood the greater percentage of the net money after fees and costs would go in trust for the benefit of Jeff. Betty would only be allowed to take funds from the account that were for the benefit of Jeff. No moneys were to be used for Betty's own personal use. Although Betty said she understood, I had my doubts and I knew any settlement agreed to would have to be in writing from Betty as well as Jeff.

As expected, I received a phone call from the manufacturer's representative that they wanted to have a meeting to try to resolve this case before spending the money for attorney fees and costs preparing and going through a week-long trial. Unexpectedly this phone call came from an employee of the manufacturer and not its attorneys.

The meeting was scheduled at my office for 1 p.m. on a date that was about ten weeks before the scheduled trial. The manufacturer's representative advised me that he would allow only four hours for our meeting as he would have to catch a plane at 6:30 p.m. to return home. The inference was clear to me that they wanted to settle that day, and if there were no settlement they would prepare to defend this case at trial.

The date for the settlement negotiation was 3 days from the phone call. I contacted Betty and told her about the telephone call and requested that on the day of the meeting she standby for a phone call and be at a location where there was a fax machine so I could fax all offers to her and her acceptance or rejection of any offer, would be in writing. I did not want to take any chance that what I said about settlement would be misinterpreted. I then advised my partner, Don, of this meeting and made sure he would be available. Don was familiar with the facts of this case and would be a tremendous asset in the negotiations. He has a unique ability in reading people and is very good at knowing when the risk is too great to continue negotiating. I, on the other hand, have been known to be overly optimistic on the cases I handle and take a little more risk than I should. Fortunately I have not been wrong in most cases. Don and I have worked well together over the many years he and I have been partners and I knew his participation would be a great asset.

Before the meeting, I called my expert, Boulter Kelsey, and asked whether he had been able to get the tractor he had purchased to jump into gear from neutral while it was idling as had been described by Rick in his deposition. Boulter said he had done everything he could to see if he was able to have the tractor jump into gear from neutral and was unsuccessful. He went on to state off the record it was his best guess that Rick had unintentionally left the gear in the forward position in his rush to get off the tractor and move Jeff from harms way when the tractor continued forward running over Rick's foot and then riding over the poor child lying on the blanket in the sun totally unaware that his life would be changed forever through no fault of his own.

The only theory I had to present to the jury was the manufacturer's failure to add the automatic shut-off device that would be placed under the seat and cut the motor off once the driver got up off the seat. This device, which only cost 75 cents, would have prevented the injuries Jeff suffered had they been willing to install it.

The meeting with the two representatives started on time on the date it was scheduled. The two men appeared in their late forties and early fifties, well dressed, and each carrying a small briefcase.

They started off reminding Don and me that these discussions need to be completed within the four-hour deadline and they would leave and inform their attorneys to prepare for trial if the case did not settle. They went on to state that they were here to pay money for Jeff's injuries but in no way would they admit any wrongdoing or that their tractor was defective. They also insisted that any settlement made be confidential. I told them that those conditions would not be a problem but I would still need my clients' consent.

John, who appeared to be the one in charge, then simply said they were prepared to pay $700,000 for a full release.

Don reminded John and Steve, the other representative, that since Jeff was a minor and any settlement would have to be approved by the Court and an estate would have to be opened for Jeff so the funds could be deposited in this estate until Jeff reached 21 years of age.

We then told John we would send this offer to Betty and Jeff who were waiting for our call. We excused ourselves and went into my office. Both Don and I were surprised by the amount of the opening offer. We discussed the fact that we believe they would pay up to $1 million but we were not sure they would pay more. We also discussed the problem we may have with Betty. She may not be willing to reject this offer.

I called Betty and advised her of the condition that John set out and she agreed. I then told Betty that the representative made an opening offer of $700,000 and I heard Betty scream out "oh, my God." She started to cry and, after a couple of minutes still breathing heavy, she asked, "what should we do?" I told Betty to reject this offer and give me written authority to settle for $1,950,000. I told her I would fax this $700,000 offer to her and she should write on the document "I reject this offer and authorize you to demand $1,950,000." I told her to sign this statement, have Jeff sign it, and fax it back to my office immediately, which she agreed to do.

Don and I went back into my conference room and I told John and Steve that my clients had verbally rejected their offer of $700,000 and I was waiting for written confirmation. I also told them I would be getting authority to make a counter demand and will be receiving this in writing. My secretary knocked on the door and brought in the fax returned by Betty and Jeff, which they had properly completed and signed.

I gave a copy of Betty and Jeff's rejection of the $700,000 initial offer to each John and Steve with the counter demand of $1,950,000. Steve was irritated somewhat and said as much. Steve let us know that he was very familiar with the design of this model and there was no defective design as we alleged. Steve went on to state that this particular tractor could never have jumped into gear from neutral as described by Rick in his deposition. This is exactly what my expert had told me. Steve went on to state that in all probability Rick had not completely taken the gear from forward to neutral and the gear moved back into forward which then caused the tractor to run over baby Jeff. John then said they believe their attorney would be able to convince a jury that all of Jeff's injuries were due to Rick's negligence and not the design. Steve let it be known that he had been heavily involved in the design of this particular model.

I responded by stating that even if a jury believed that Rick did not fully put the gear into neutral, they still had a problem in failing to install the automatic shut-off valve under the seat of the tractor. Had they installed this device, Jeff would never had suffered these terrible injuries and we wouldn't be here. Don, my partner, then said that the issue of liability is for the jury and this meeting was simply a settlement discussion. Don asked them to stick to our agenda as we were limited in time and as a result, the representative asked if they could be alone for about 15 minutes to decide if they wanted to respond to the counter demand. Don was extremely valuable as he handled all key motions, drafting of pleadings, and the strategy for keeping this case in Missouri.

While the representatives from the manufacturer were meeting, Don and I were trying to anticipate the next offer from them and how we should respond. We had hoped to settle north of $1,000,000, but were not sure how far they were willing to go before calling off settlement discussions.

The two men came back into the conference room and said they had flown to St. Louis to settle the case, but were prepared to litigate if our settlement demands were excessive.

John then handed me a folded paper. I opened it slowly and saw written $875,000. I informed the men that we would fax this to our clients and hopefully have a response in about 15 minutes.

As soon as we faxed the new offer to the clients with instructions to reject this offer, Don and I discussed the proper response. I felt quite certain that they would go to $1,000,000 but how much beyond was an unknown. Also I was getting nervous as to whether our client had the stomach to reject the $875,000. I would have felt better had the client been with me as it would have been easier with direct contact and I could better judge the reaction Betty would have to each offer. Finally the fax came back from Betty with her and Jeff's signature rejecting this latest offer. In addition, there was an inquiry as to how much did I think they were willing to pay to settle this case. The truth was I had no idea other than I had a feeling it would exceed $1,000,000.

Don and I discussed the next demand we would make. It had to send a clear message we wanted at least a million but not be so high that it could end negotiations. Don and I thought our next demand should be reduced to $1,550,000. I called Betty and asked her to send me a note signed by her and Jeff agreeing to make another demand for the new figure. I advised her that I think they would respond by going to $1,000,000 and then we would have to seriously discuss what would be the settlement figure we could not refuse. Betty agreed with that strategy but, once again, she asked me how much money she would receive from any settlement reached. I was bothered because on multiple occasions I had told Betty that any settlement funds were for Jeff's benefit. I had told her she could use the funds for food, clothing, transportation, and any of Jeff's needs. I was becoming concerned that Betty was going to be a problem.

I received the signed document from Betty authorizing the new demand. Don and I entered the conference room and I passed the new demand to the manufacturer's main negotiator. As he was reviewing the settlement figure, I told him that my client is interested in resolving this case but it cannot be done at the amount that would not be sufficient to take care of Jeff for the rest of his life, which could be another sixty-five years. I advised them that I have little room if any for further negotiation. John replied that he and Steve needed about 30 minutes to discuss our latest demand and he would come back with his "best and last offer" to attempt to settle this case. There was only about an hour left on their deadline, which meant if they were serious about this time constraint we would only have about a half hour left after their next offer to attempt to settle this case.

I called Betty and told her that we should be getting a new offer in the next 30 minutes and we are getting very close to a final discussion.

The time passed slowly. I was thinking nervously about all the possible scenarios. The worst scenario would have been if they only increased their offer by $100,000 to stay under a $1,000,000. There would be a very good chance that Betty would accept this offer and leave much more money on the table.

After about twenty minutes, John came into my office and said he was ready to continue. Don and I met him in the conference room where we were seated directly across each other in the middle of a long thirty-foot dark conference table.

John explained that they had talked to their attorney as to the merits of the case, but as in most cases there was no guarantee that they could successfully defend this case. Since there is very little time left to complete these settlement negotiations, they were prepared to make their final offer to settle this case. John went on to state if the client rejects this final offer then it will be withdrawn and they will advise their attorney to prepare for trial and let a jury make the decision. Then about 15 seconds of silence, which seemed to me like an eternity, John opened his notebook, glanced down, paused for a couple of seconds, and replied: We will offer

"$1,150,000." My heart immediately started beating faster and I felt my hands feeling sweaty. I hoped I would not show my excitement when I responded that I thought they were sincere in their offer, but I cannot be certain it would be acceptable to my client. As we had done with all prior offers, I advised the men that I would advise my client and return as quickly as I could. The time left for negotiating was just under 20 minutes.

Don and I left the conference room and were discussing how to respond. We both believed the client would accept this offer. The challenge facing us is could we ask for more and risk them withdrawing the offer and could we advise the client to take this risk. From the client's perspective, this incident was over 14 years ago. The client had two or three previous attorneys who could not get Betty and Jeff one penny for this horrendous injury. Now, for the first time, they have been offered over a million dollars. Would it be a smart strategy to risk this offer to gain an additional $100,000? I would discuss this with Betty and Jeff and let them decide with my assistance.

I reached Betty, who sounded very anxious and upset. She was concerned because of the length of time that passed since our last conversation. I explained to Betty that the representatives were taking extra time to determine their final offer. I barely said the settlement amount when I heard Betty scream for joy. Then the next words out of her mouth were "when do I get my money?" I told Betty in very strong terms that this was not her money. It was to be put into a fund for Jeff's needs after all fees and costs were paid. These funds were to be controlled by a probate court first in Missouri and then in her state until Jeff reaches majority, 21 years old.

I went on to explain to Betty that there was a chance I could get them to pay more money, but it would be at the risk of losing the settlement offer. Betty said she would not risk losing the offer of $1,150,000 and wants to accept the offer. I advised Betty to send me a fax agreeing to accept the settlement of no less than $1,150,000. I reminded her that both she and Jeff needed to date, sign, and put the time on the acceptance. I then told her to wait exactly 10 minutes before she faxed the acceptance to me. Betty agreed.

I immediately went back into the conference room and told John my client was thinking about the final offer and was going to discuss with other people before making her decision.

I then told John that I advised the client that I felt a jury would award Jeff over $1,500,000 but with a trial and an appeal it may take several more years before Jeff saw any money.

I suggested to John that I would recommend $1,350,000 to settle the case if my client rejects the last offer, as I suggested her to do.

There was still 5 minutes left before Betty would fax her response to the last offer. I was hoping to squeeze more money from the manufacturer to help Jeff for his future needs. There was only about 12 minutes left to negotiate a settlement.

John looked at me, not sure if my client would reject the last offer, trying to read something in my face as to whether I would truly advise my client to reject their last offer.

After studying me as we stared at each other for two long minutes, John finally said, "I will pay $1,250,000 and no more. Take it or leave it." I reached over the table with my outstretched hand and said, "John, my client accepts your offer." I told John to have his attorney prepare the necessary settlement documents and I will open an estate for Jeff in which the settlement funds would be deposited for the sole use of Jeff's needs. The Court would appoint a guardian until the funds will be transferred to Iowa Probate Court in the county Jeff resides. After attorney fees and expenses, Jeff will have a sizeable estate. It was important that the funds are invested safely without risk and Betty has no access to these funds.

Within 30 days the estate was opened, the settlement checks for attorney fees and costs were given to me, and the balance deposited in Jeff's bank account controlled by the guardian appointed by the Court. Jeff's bank account exceeded over three quarter of a million dollars. I had a great feeling of a job well done on an extremely difficult case. I felt Betty and Jeff were very happy with the results.

It turned out that I was dead wrong. Several weeks after Jeff's estate was transferred to the Probate Court in Iowa, I received a letter from the Missouri Bar Disciplinary Counsel. Betty had made a formal complaint against me alleging that the settlement I reached for Jeff had not been voluntarily agreed to. As I read the complaint filed by Betty, I became angry and felt betrayed by someone I had helped obtain a substantial sum of money for her son where others had failed. Rather than being thankful, Betty was making false accusations against me in writing to the Missouri Bar.

Betty alleged that I had threatened to have Jeff taken from her if she had not accepted the offer. She stated I was more interested in getting a fee rather than a higher jury award if I went to trial.

Fortunately I had all offers and rejections in writing as well as the final acceptance of the last offer. Early in my legal career, I learned that everything with a client needed to be in writing, no matter how long you knew the client. What I learned early on is "that if it is not in writing, it never happened."

Evidently Betty was so angry when she finally realized she could not get Jeff's money, she made up lies to try and embarrass me.

I responded to the complaint with all the letters and faxes I had exchanged with Betty, which clearly showed the truth. My response filed with the Disciplinary Committee was timely filed. Two weeks later, I received a letter from the Disciplinary Committee clearing me of any wrongdoing; however, I still had a complaint on my record with the Missouri Bar Association.

Prologue

This story continued after the complaint filed by Betty. About 5 years after the complaint filed by Betty, I received a phone call from Jeff. He was now 22 years old and had complete control of his money. He was living at home with his mom and her boyfriend and he said his mom took about $175,000 from his bank account and left town with her boyfriend. Jeff just felt so betrayed by his mom since, at her request, he added her name to his bank accounts. I felt so sorry for Jeff, not just for the loss of funds, but the loss of the faith he had in his mother.

CHAPTER IV

FATAL REUNION

I had represented this particular insurance company and its insureds for over 10 years. They had retained me to defend cases not only pending in Missouri, but across the U.S. This company specialized in insuring automobile dealers and companies in the automotive industry.

I received a call from the head of claims telling me that he had a serious case that will be tried in Kansas City, Missouri, in six months and he wanted me to be lead counsel. They insured the automobile dealer and its employees for general liability with policy limits of $1,000,000. I had worked with Dave Sands for over five years; he would call infrequently, but when he did, it was always a problem case. Dave requested that I meet him at his office tomorrow afternoon and we could discuss the details. I told him I would see him there at 1 p.m.

Kansas City was an easy 3½-hour drive from St. Louis and I reached Dave's office about 12:30 p.m. It is always important to me to be early for every appointment if possible. I only had to wait about 15 minutes when Dave arrived with the adjuster, Marla White, who was the person handling this case. As is the custom in most insurance companies, the primary adjuster has authority to settle up to a nominal amount such as $50,000. After the $50,000, the case goes to a senior adjuster who has authority up to $200,000. In the event there is a potential for a loss exceeding $200,000, the case is reviewed by the home office in Kansas City.

As a result of the facts of this case and the potential of a verdict loss larger than $200,000, this case found its way to the desk of Dave Sands.

Dave ushered Marla and me into one of the conference rooms on the 6th floor. Marla had her complete file, which included the investigation, pleadings, and correspondence from the attorney who was defending this case. Marla advised that she had told the local attorney that I would enter my appearance on behalf of the employee and he would stay on as attorney for the dealership. The two attorneys were necessary because of a potential conflict since the employee may not have coverage if the facts showed he was not acting within the course and scope of his employment when the accident occurred.

Marla then went on to discuss the facts of this case. The employee, John Hart, was a salesman with the dealership and had been with them for about 18 months. As is the practice of this particular dealership, each salesman was given a new car to use. The purpose was to have people view the car as the salesman drove around the area, allow the salesman to let people test drive the vehicle and they would not necessarily have to come to the dealership. Also, it was part of the salesman's salary package.

On the day of the accident, John had worked until 3 p.m. on a Saturday. He left the dealership and went to the home of a friend who was home from college. They had planned to meet at 4 p.m. When John arrived at his friend's house, he met another individual who attended the same college with John's friend. John was the oldest of the three, being 23. The other two were 21 or 22 years of age.

The three young men started drinking. First they consumed a case of beer. After a couple of hours, they consumed a second case. John remembered driving the three of them to a liquor store where they bought two bottles of scotch and returned to the home of John's friend where the three of them consumed the second case of beer and maybe a third as well as the two bottles of scotch. John did not have any other recollection of the facts that night.

Marla went on to review the police report that showed John's car had left the road at approximately 1:30 a.m. the next morning and apparently rolled over several times. The report surmised that the car had been traveling at an extremely high rate of speed in a 45-mile-per-hour zone at a sharp curve and left the highway. All three occupants were thrown from the vehicle and at least one or maybe two had been thrown into a tree. Only John had survived. The other two were dead when the police arrived.

The police had found bone fragments embedded in one of the trees at the scene but, at the time of the report, the police could not identify to which man the fragments belonged.

John was taken to a nearby hospital where he had blood samples taken which showed the level of blood alcohol in his system far exceeded the legal limit. John denied that he was the driver of the vehicle at the time of the accident although he did admit that he drove to and from the liquor store that evening. The initial investigation by the local police was unable to determine who was driving the vehicle at the time of this accident.

The suit I was requested to defend was brought by the mother of John's friend, who I learned was just about three months shy of his 22nd birthday. The young man was single with no children or siblings and his father had passed away a few years earlier.

Dave said that the attorney for the plaintiff, the mother, has demanded $600,000 for the wrongful death of the young man and the insurance company's last formal offer had been $150,000. The next court date was a case management conference about 60 days from our meeting. I told Dave I would review the file, meet with my client, and then meet with the attorney for the dealership. I told Dave and Marla that I would be ready for the case management conference and for the trial. Dave told me he would be handling the file from here on and all my instructions will come from him.

After I left Dave's office, I called my new client. He was working until 7 p.m. that night and would meet up at the dealership. When I arrived at the dealership at 6:45 p.m., I asked the receptionist to see John Hart. She pointed him out to me, indicating he was with a customer but should be through shortly. John was sitting at a metal desk in a small cubicle facing toward the showroom floor. Sitting in front of him were two nicely dressed individuals whom I would guess were married.

John had a clean look about him with wavy black hair. His smile seemed sincere and he was apparently displaying good eye contact to the couple in front of him. I immediately thought a jury would like him just from first sight before they heard any facts. I waited about 25 minutes before John completed his business with the young couple.

John stood up and shook hands with both customers and I noted that he touched each of their shoulders while shaking their hand. A warm gesture, I thought. I also noticed John was about 6'2" and slightly built. When John was alone, I walked over to him and introduced myself.

We exited the dealership and went to a nearby restaurant where we spent about 90 minutes discussing facts that John would rather forget. John admitted that he was pretty intoxicated at the time of the accident, but he was insistent that he was not the driver. John was devastated by the death of his friend and the other young man whom he had just met. John admitted that he was reprimanded by his employer for this incident, but his employer believed John about not being the driver and, as a result, John was able to keep his job. Had John admitted to driving, he would have violated company policy about driving while intoxicated and been terminated from his employment. More importantly, if the police could prove that John was the driver, he probably would have been charged with vehicular manslaughter and faced possible jail time. In any event, no criminal charges had been brought and it was 13 months since this tragic event.

I attended the case management conference in the Civil Courts building in downtown Kansas City, Missouri. The judge was a woman who had been a circuit judge for a little over five years. She knew both the plaintiff's attorney and the attorney for the dealership. I introduced myself and I was treated cordially.

The plaintiff's attorney wore a sport coat and was well dressed. I noted that he wore casual but expensive loafers with tassels.

The judge asked if we could settle the case since this was such a tragedy and there was a risk in letting a jury decide this case. I let the judge know that my client is interested in settling this case but plaintiff's attorney has made what I thought was an excessive demand for settlement. I advised the judge in my opinion any verdict received against my client would be reduced by a percentage of fault of the plaintiff's son. I also reminded the judge that plaintiff would still have to prove that my client was the driver of the vehicle.

After the case management conference, the plaintiff's attorney asked if I had time to discuss this case and see if we could resolve some of the legal issues regarding introduction of documents, such as the police report and the toxicology results of my client's blood level that had shown his level of intoxication. He also wanted to see if there was any possibility of settlement. I responded that I would be happy to sit down with him and discuss any topic he desired. Plaintiff's attorney was familiar with a quiet sandwich shop not far from the courthouse.

Plaintiff's attorney, Tom Hecht, initiated the conversation and started by telling me what a successful trial lawyer he has been over the last 25 or 30 years. He was a partner in a small 18-person firm. The firm's biggest client, he let me know, was the Kansas City Chief's who, at that time, had a pretty good NFL football team.

I let Tom know that I had defended many cases all over the country for this particular insurance company and I had my share of successes. I went on to state that I would relate any new demand that he made to my client and his insurance carrier, but I could not suggest any settlement amount. I told Tom I was simply a messenger.

Tom said he would have an expert who will testify that based on the evidence found at the scene of the position of where the bodies were found, he concluded that the driver of the car was my client. I was not surprised by this disclosure because the insurance on my client was the deepest pocket. I did think there was an 80 percent chance I could exclude this expert's testimony as it would be based on the most speculative theories in my opinion. I knew based on my experience that for enough money you could retain an expert to support any position.

I discussed the issue of damages with Tom and told him he had no evidence that the deceased had lived for any period of time after the accident and therefore he could not recover for pain and suffering. I let Tom know that in my opinion the only damages were the funeral bill and loss of love and affection. There was no evidence that the deceased had been supporting his widowed mom. After all, the deceased was in school and in all probability the plaintiff was contributing to the support of the deceased. I told plaintiff's attorney that I did not believe the verdict would come close to his demand of $600,000. I also stated that I felt a jury would find a percentage of fault against the deceased for being a part of this excessive drinking that evening and was a major participant in the evening's events. Tom and I parted after about an hour and a half of sparring verbally with each other no closer to a resolution.

As the months passed and we were two weeks from trial, Dave called me asking if I heard from plaintiff's attorney regarding settlement. I advised Dave that as far as I knew plaintiff's demand was still $600,000. Dave asked me to call plaintiff's attorney and see if he was willing to settle the case for $200,000. I told Dave I was reluctant to increase the offer without a reduced demand from plaintiff. Dave was insistent that I make the offer immediately.

Reluctantly I called plaintiff's attorney and told Tom that in a last ditch effort to resolve this matter, I have been authorized to extend an offer of $200,000 to settle this matter. Tom said he would present this offer to his client, but he would advise her to reject the offer. I asked Tom to make any counter demand he felt comfortable with if his client rejected the latest offer.

I heard from Tom the next afternoon with the rejection as promised. Tom did, however, make a lower demand to one-half a million dollars.

I called Dave and told him of the rejection of the $200,000 offer and the new demand of $500,000. I suggested to Dave that he should not increase his offer as I thought this would be the high range of any jury verdict reached against my client. I reminded Dave that infrequently there were what are referred to as "runaway" verdicts, but I did not think this was one of those cases. Each of the young men had voluntarily been participants in a wild drinking binge and any one of them could have driven the car that evening. Each of the three, in my opinion, were equally at fault that dreadful evening. In my opinion, Dave should not make another offer and just try the case to conclusion unless plaintiff reduced her demand to $250,000.

I drove up to Kansas City to meet with the claims committee Friday before trial. The claims committee was made up of seven individuals, each who headed a division of the country as the Executive Claims Manager. The purpose of this meeting was to discuss the negotiations to date and the risk of going to trial Monday. I presented all the significant facts and gave my thoughts regarding liability and chances of a defendant's verdict. I also gave my opinion as to the range of an unfavorable verdict for plaintiff. Each person at the meeting provided input, and it was decided to make no offer and see the makeup of the jury after *voir dire*.

That Monday morning, the attorneys met in the judge's chambers at 9 a.m. to argue all the preliminary motions, including my motion to strike plaintiff's expert who put my client at the wheel when the accident happened. I lost, the motion to strike plaintiff's expert. This ruling was not really unexpected since plaintiff could not make a case against my client without this expert's testimony.

The *voir dire* took most of the morning and, while a brief recess was taken for the attorney to make their required jury strikes, Dave unexpectedly approached the plaintiff's attorney and increased the settlement offer to $250,000 and said it was his final offer. This offer was rejected by plaintiff's attorney. I then told Dave to leave the courthouse and let's just try the case and let the jury reach a verdict.

The required strikes were made and the first 12 jurors were seven women and five men. There were two alternates, both men.

The first day and a half the plaintiff's attorney's evidence was the background of my client's employment with the dealership and his use of the demo car he was provided by the dealership. He also had the investigating officer describe in detail the accident scene and the bone fragments he found embedded in the tree. The jury also was shown the photos of the vehicle, which was a series of twisted steel and broken glass. The interior was twisted and torn and you could not tell where the front seat was separated from the back seat. Apparently from the pictures, it would be difficult for anyone to survive the crash had the passengers remained in the vehicle.

In the third day of trial, plaintiff put on his expert to explain to the jury how he was able to reach the opinion that my client was the driver. This expert, during direct examination, laid out to the jury each and every fact that supported his opinion. During my cross-examination, I thought I had this expert back down on some of his conclusions and even had the expert admit that it was slightly possible that either of the other two boys could have been the driver; but in the end, he said his opinion with reasonable reconstruction certainty was that my client was the driver of that automobile when the crash occurred. I pointed out to the jury that this testimony cost $10,000. The last witness in the plaintiff's case was the deceased's mother. The attorney for the plaintiff wanted the jury to see the mother of this young man and feel her loss. This was a very good decision for the plaintiff's case and I knew the jury would be impressed.

Plaintiff was on the stand for about an hour and a half as she went through her deceased son's early childhood, his teenage years, and his start of college. She testified as to how good of a son he was and how she would get calls from him almost five days a week when he was away in college. The mother was soft spoken with tears in her eyes as she painted the picture of a near-perfect son who was now gone from her life. She told the jury she would never have grandchildren nor would she have the pleasure of watching her young son get married and have a family. I felt the jury truly liked this woman and could feel her pain. I knew that I had to be very careful with my cross-exam, which would start right after lunch.

As the jury was being seated to start the afternoon of the third day of trial, I sensed they were focusing on my client as if ready to find against him.

The judge was seated and announced that I could start my cross-examination of the plaintiff. I stood up and walked slowly to the left of the witness stand so I would be facing the jury as I questioned the mother.

Before I started my questions, I looked at the witness and told her how sorry I was for her loss. I went on to say that I could not ever imagine the pain she must be feeling as I have not personally experienced the loss of a child and I was the father of two wonderful children.

The witness seemed more relaxed as tears welled up not only in her eyes but mine as well. I was sincere in these statements and thought about the feelings I would experience if the deceased had been one of my own.

Over the course of the next 15 minutes, the mother told the jury in response to my questions that she had always talked to her son about not drinking and driving. More importantly related to the facts of this case, she always told her son never to get into a car as a passenger with someone you know had been drinking. The witness agreed that she had been diligent in discussing the dangers of getting into a vehicle with a driver who had been drinking. As far as the mother knew, her son followed her advice. She agreed that in this one instance her son ignored her advice and risked his life when he entered the car that night no matter who was driving the car.

The mother's testimony supported my strongest defense that if the jury found that my client was the driver the deceased was charged with a percentage of fault and the verdict, if any, against my client should be diminished by that percentage assessed against the deceased for entering the vehicle knowing the driver was severely intoxicated well above the legal limit.

Another important point was that I had the witness admit that she received no monetary support from the deceased. Further, the mother admitted that she rarely saw her son since he was in college for the last three years and, when school recessed for the summer months, he spent most of his time hanging out with friends, which was typical for this age group.

During my portion of the case, the only witness I called was my client. The client told the jury that he was the driver when the three went to pick up the alcohol but has no recollection of who was driving at the time of the accident. He went on to state that he would not have driven because it was against the rules of his employer. He also admitted that it was against the employer's rules to let someone else drive the company car. He had no explanation as to how either of the other persons would have taken his keys. He admitted if he were the driver he would have been too intoxicated to drive, but insisted he would not have knowingly driven the car that night.

The trial now moved to closing arguments. Both plaintiff and defendants had presented all their evidence with no rebuttal evidence from plaintiff.

The judge had given plaintiff 45 minutes each to present closing arguments. The defendants had to split 45 minutes and I convinced the dealer's attorney to let me take 35 of those minutes, to which he readily agreed.

The plaintiff's attorney told the jury about this terrible loss to the mother and how she would never experience his marriage or hug his children or ever hug her son again. He then went on to describe the horrific accident showing the gruesome photos. At the end of his opening statement, he asked the jury for $1,000,000.

As I started my closing argument, I reminded the jury that they could not be influenced by one's sympathy for the plaintiff. That they must pay attention to the facts. I pointed out that the plaintiff did not suffer any pecuniary loss except for the funeral bill and cost of the ambulance. I said that there was no evidence that the deceased would ever marry and if he did that he ever would have children. I then went on to state that other than the plaintiff's expert, who was paid $10,000 for his opinion, there is no evidence that my client was behind the wheel just before the accident.

I told the jury that I would not suggest an amount if they believed my client was the driver, but if they found against my client, whatever amount they determined should take into account that the deceased did not provide any monetary support to the plaintiff.

I then asked the jury to find the deceased a percentage of fault as he voluntarily either drove or was a passenger when he and the driver, if he was not driving, were knowingly impaired that evening. The jury then left the jury box to deliberate this case. The jury took over three and a half hours. During that time, Dave called numerous times anxiously awaiting the verdict. After two hours, Dave could not wait any longer and came down to the courthouse to wait until a verdict was reached.

Then, about 7 p.m., the bell rang twice. There was a verdict. As the jury filed into the jury box, the foreman held the verdict in his hands. It seemed like forever until the verdict was given to the bailiff, who walked across the courtroom floor and handed the verdict form to the judge. The judge unfolded the form and read to himself. Then the judge asked the jury to stand and read the following: verdict in favor of the plaintiff against my client and in favor of the dealer. The damages were $100,000 with the deceased being comparatively at fault for 40 percent and the driver 60 percent. The net effect was a $60,000 verdict for the plaintiff.

This is a prime example of the risk an attorney takes as well as the client in letting the jury decide. In my opinion, the plaintiff's attorney was too greedy and would have served his client better had he accepted the final offer of $250,000.

Although this was a big success for the insurance carrier, my thoughts went to the mother who not only lost her son, but lost her case and had to relive the events of the death of her son.

CHAPTER V

IS SUICIDE INSURABLE?

It was a beautiful, sunny day in August. There was a cloudless blue sky. I was having lunch on the 24th floor at the Top of the 7s with a good friend and client. Chuck was the president and chief operating officer of a family-owned flour business and had taken over running of the business from his father two years earlier. Chuck's father had actually succeeded Chuck's grandfather, who started the business 70 years earlier.

The restaurant had large windows with northern and eastern exposures and you could see toward the east, twelve miles away, the St. Louis Arch high above the mighty Mississippi River. The restaurant had a large bar in the middle of the room with tables on the main floor as well as a section referred to as the Terrace, which rose about 3 feet above the main floor. Chuck and I were sitting on the terrace enjoying a nice lunch and discussing some of the issues he was having with his father who was at the office every day.

Even though Chuck's father was supposed to be retired, his father was continuing to second guess many of Chuck's decisions. Chuck was a very outgoing person and made friends easily. In his first two years of running the family business, sales had increased 40%.

As I was listening to my good friend discuss the issue he was having with his father, my gaze was looking northward and I could see airplanes landing at Lambert Field, which was about seven miles away. I also could see the tall building across the street to the west.

As I was looking over Chuck's shoulder and half listening to his problem with his father, I noticed an object that appeared to be thrown from a 14th floor window of the building across the street. The object appeared to be a chair, but I couldn't be certain. About 30 seconds later, I saw a body come through the same window and drop out of sight.

I immediately jumped and ran to the window about 10 feet away leaving Chuck talking to no one. As I approached the large plate glass window, I heard some people screaming and others who had seen this terrible scene also coming toward the window.

As I observed the scene below on this beautiful summer day, I looked down on the roof of the parking garage which was four stories high and saw a motionless body and a piece of furniture. It was a terrible sight. At this time, I had no facts as to the cause of this person's fall from the window of the building across the street.

By this time, my friend Chuck had also come to the window and viewed the same scene. The crowd of people engrossed in viewing the motionless body was noticeably upset and some appeared to be weeping, although obviously they could not identify the body on the roof across the street.

It was interesting that many people left without finishing their lunches, but a large number went back to their tables to complete their meal. Chuck and I had no desire for food. I signed the check and we left to return to our offices and go about our everyday, normal activities. I would imagine that the majority of people who had witnessed this tragic event said a brief prayer. Like me, I am sure that everyone shortly would go on with their lives with no thought of this poor individual on the roof or any family this person left behind.

Approximately eight months after that tragic event, I received a call from a woman who had been referred to me by an insurance broker I had previously represented. The broker had specialized in life insurance and health insurance for large groups. The woman had a problem with a life insurance policy that had been purchased by her late husband almost three years earlier.

The woman, named Ann, had recently been widowed. That is how she started our initial interview. Ann was about 57 years old and had two children, a girl about twenty-eight and a son who was a senior in high school. She and her late husband had moved from Cleveland, Ohio, almost three years ago. Her husband, Fred, had been with an investment firm for over 15 years and had an offer to go with one of the large brokerage companies in St. Louis. The decision was made to take this offer and move the family to St. Louis.

Ann went on to state that as part of their estate planning, Fred had decided to purchase a variable life insurance policy with limits of $250,000. The insurance agent was a dear friend and a very famous football player for the Cleveland Browns who had been retired for over ten years. The process for obtaining the policy started a few months before the offer to accept the position in St. Louis was finalized. By the time the policy was finally delivered to Fred, he had already accepted the new position in St. Louis. The insurance broker was aware that Fred was moving from Cleveland to St. Louis some four weeks before the policy was finalized and delivered to Fred.

Ann went on to describe how Fred loved his new job at first. They had a wonderful two-story home in a nice neighborhood and their son was enjoying his new school. Jack, the son, had made friends easily and was active in school events and played baseball for his high school. The change to a new job, a new city, and a new school was a success for Fred, Ann, and Jack.

Ann then went on and tears welled in her eyes as she discussed the change in Fred almost a year at his new job. Things were going from bad to worse as he wasn't producing like his new employers expected. He had become more depressed each week. He had started drinking more and spent more time alone. About three months before his death, he had gone for professional help but after two visits refused to return. Unbeknownst to Ann, Fred had been terminated from his job and had been given two weeks to transfer all his files and he was given three months severance pay. Then on the second to last of his remaining days at his job, Fred decided to take his life by leaping from the fourteenth floor office he occupied. The office was located in Clayton, a business and residential community about 12 miles west of downtown St. Louis. As Ann was describing her husband's suicide, I realized that this was what I had witnessed that day in August when I was having lunch with my good friend Chuck. I told Ann that I had actually witnessed her husband's suicide and I was so sorry for her loss. Ann started crying and I felt that fate had brought her to my office. Although Ann asked me to describe what I had observed, I thought it was best to tell her I only observed her husband's body after the event and I could not see much from where I was located. Still, Ann kept asking me to tell her anything I could about that terrible day. I kept my description to a bare minimum as I knew there was nothing positive I could describe to Ann. After about thirty minutes, Ann composed herself and she went on to describe the problems she was having in trying to collect the insurance proceeds from Fred's $250,000 life insurance policy.

Ann related how her insurance broker friend in Cleveland helped her complete the claim form and send it with a copy of the death certificate to the life insurance company. After a few weeks, Ann received a letter from the insurance carrier denying her claim for the reason that the policy of life insurance purchased by Fred had a clause regarding suicide by the insured in the first two years the policy was in force. Since Fred's death was ruled a suicide, and at the time of Fred's demise two years had not passed from the inception, so the insurance carrier refused to pay the policy limits. The letter ended by the vice president stating she was sincerely sorry for the loss but she was unable by the terms of the policy to pay the policy limits.

Ann's friend and insurance broker told her that he had checked with one of his friends who specializes in insurance law in Cleveland and was told by this lawyer that unfortunately the insurance carrier had the right to deny her claim because of the suicide provision in Fred's life insurance policy.

I told Ann that I would be willing to represent her and I would have to do some research. I would have her sign some documents to allow me to get a copy of the complete file from the insurance company, which would include the application, the medical exam, and the underwriting, as well as any other pertinent documents. I told Ann that if we had to file suit against the insurance carrier it could become expensive. As I do with most of my clients on these types of cases, I gave Ann the choice of retaining my service by payment of an hourly rate with a large retainer or agree to a percentage of any recovery with all costs to be paid by her. Ann said that she would not be able to pay attorney fees and would feel more comfortable paying a percentage of any recovery, with no fee obligation if no moneys were recovered from the insurance carrier. After all the necessary papers were signed, I told Ann I would start to work on her file and keep her informed on all developments.

I opened a new file for Ann's claim. I dictated a formal request to the insurance carrier for a copy of all documents relevant to the purchasing of the policy. Among the documents I requested were the application, medical exam, their underwriting documents, and anything the insurance carrier relied on to determine to write the policy of insurance on Fred's life. A copy of this letter was sent to Ann so she could see the progress on her claim.

It took a little over two weeks before I received a large package from the insurance carrier including the documents requested as well as some other internal documents which were responsive to my request but which I hadn't been familiar with and were probably used solely for this particular carrier.

I informed Ann that I had received the documents and it would take me a few days to review them. There were approximately 75 pages of documents that needed to be reviewed. I also told Ann that my partner Lori was almost completed with her research on the issue of the suicide provision which was part of Fred's life insurance policy.

In going through the application, I found nothing that was out of the ordinary. Fred showed his address in Cleveland. All of the questions pertaining to a male applicant had been answered.

One interesting issue that my partner Lori was researching was which state law applied in this case. Fred purchased the policy as a resident of Cleveland, Ohio. Fred died as a resident of Chesterfield, Missouri. The legal question is which state law applied to this case. I remember years ago in my second year of law school I took a Conflicts of Law class with Professor Callahan. My recollection of the professor was that he enjoyed putting his students on the spot. He would phrase his questions in such a vague manner it was difficult to determine a correct response to his questions. Most students would keep their heads down looking into their open book not wanting to make eye contact with the professor for fear of being called upon and embarrassed in front of the whole class. I remember one such occasion which happened to me and a fellow student, Ed. This occurred over 25 years ago and I remember it like it was yesterday. It went as follows: "Sanford." I picked my head up from the book and felt my heart start to pound. "Yes, sir," I replied. "Do you believe in the old adage 'The early bird gets the worm?'" In my almost two-year law school experience, there was no case I had read or law book I had studied that prepared me for this question. After what seemed like an hour, but only three minutes, I finally said, "Yes, sir," having no idea what I was responding to. Then quickly Professor Callahan turned to his left to the other side of the class and said, "Ed, do you believe in the old adage, 'Look before you leap?'" Like me, Ed paused for a few minutes and replied, "Yes, sir." Then, without any warning, the professor turned back to me and said, "Sanford, your classmate Ed disagrees with you. Can you tell us what you based your decision on?" I was looking straight ahead with probably a blank stare and my heart racing so fast that I simply replied, "No, sir, I cannot." With that Professor Callahan stood up, slammed his notebook shut with a loud bang, and announced that the class was over as he would not teach students unprepared. This was my recollection of my Conflict of Laws class over 25 years ago. Now I am representing a client with a conflict of laws problem and the correct answer to this problem will possibly determine whether or not I am successful in representing Ann.

I had a meeting with my partner Lori, who advised me that she had completed the research on the suicide provision in Fred's policy and was available to meet with me at 4:00 p.m. and would need about an hour of my time to discuss what she concluded based upon her review of all the relevant cases.

When I walked into the conference room, Lori had two separate stacks of documents along with her legal pad with the usual underlining, notes in red, as well as circled notes and asterisks all over. I guessed that she had over twenty pages of notes.

According to Lori, her extensive research led her to conclude that the majority of cases allowed the insurance carrier to void the policy with no payment if the insured committed suicide within two years from the issue date. I immediately thought that this would prevent Ann from receiving the insurance proceeds which would be a terrible blow to Ann's hopes and expectations.

Lori, however, went on with the analysis. "It seems," she said, "that there are only two states that follow the minority view. One of those states is Missouri." The minority view allows the insurance carrier to void the policy if suicide occurs within two years of the issuance of the policy. However, the insurance carrier has the burden to prove that the insured intended to commit suicide on the date he applied for the insurance. This, of course, is an almost impossible burden for the insurance carrier to meet. I called Ann and explained to her that we have a very good chance of collecting the insurance proceeds if the laws of the state of Missouri are applicable to our claim. I told her of the two legal opinions as to the interpretation of the suicide provision of the policy, with Missouri being in the minority.

I also advised Ann that she could decide to allow us to negotiate a settlement with the insurance carrier and agree to accept less than the face value of $250,000. I told Ann that with the majority of the states construing the suicide provision adverse to our position, I didn't feel they would be willing to pay more than 50 percent and maybe not go that high in their settlement offer. I asked Ann to think for a few days about what she wanted to do and I would complete my review of the documents I had received from the insurance company.

The next day I set aside a couple hours in the morning to review the remaining documents I had not yet reviewed. I went through the medical exam questionnaire in great detail as well as the notes made by the examiner. I wanted to make certain there were no responses made by the insured that showed depression of any kind or suicidal ideation. I also wanted to make sure the examiner's notes did not reflect anything which could be interpreted about suicidal thoughts. Fortunately, there were none.

I then turned my attention to the thirty or so pages in the insurer's underwriting file. Many of the documents were internal codes about ratings and the possible premiums to consider based upon drinking, smoking, weight, as well as certain medical findings. As I was getting close to reviewing all the documents in the underwriting file, there were three typed preprinted forms that had states listed with certain provisions particular to each state. As I was turning the pages, I noticed what appeared to be a four-line black stamped notation on the page. The writing almost blended in with the preprinted paragraphs. I continued to stare for what seemed like several minutes at the stamped wording when I finally was able to make out the complete wording. The words were: "The terms of this life insurance policy shall be construed under the laws of the state of Missouri." I immediately wanted to hug the employee who placed that stamp on those pages of preprinted forms that were part of the policy. This was such a strong piece of evidence that there was no way the insurer could refuse full payment for the limits of the policy. Failure to pay the

$250,000 to Ann would make the insurance carrier subject to a bad faith claim that could cost them millions.

I called Ann and told her what I had found in the documents. I told her that she would receive the proceeds of the life insurance plus interest less legal fees.

Ann was thrilled and very appreciative and started crying as she said this is very good news, but I would prefer to have my husband back. I felt sorry for Ann's loss and told her so. I told Ann that I would write a demand letter to the insurance carrier including the Missouri case law as well as the document containing the stamp which construed the policy under Missouri law. I told Ann I would give them five business days to respond and if no timely response was received, I would file suit for the policy limits plus bad faith.

The next day I sent the demand letter by certified mail requesting a signed receipt. Three days later I received a telephone call from one of the vice presidents of the insurance carrier advising me that the company had reviewed their file and determined that they would now pay my client the $250,000 policy limit plus the interest due from date of death, which added another $2700. Then the vice president of the insurance carrier sort of chuckled and said, "If I ever find out who stamped the policy showing Missouri law applied, I will fire that person."

He let me know the check would be Fedex'd overnight and I would have it the next day. When I hung up the phone, I immediately called Ann and let her know the good news. I told her she could come to the office and we could sign the release and all of the documents needed for the insurance carrier's file. I would then prepare our office's settlement documents and write the check for Ann, which was the balance after fees.

I put down the phone and felt very satisfied that I was able to help Ann, a widow with two children, especially after Ann was advised that she could not successfully win her claim for the $250,000.

Once again it showed that a final decision should not be made until you thoroughly examine the case laws, review all the documents in detail, and analyze all the facts in a case.

I also reflected on how unusual it was that the event I witnessed, when a man committed suicide, that I would end up being the one who helped his wife and family. Coincidence or a higher power?

CHAPTER VI

THE PHANTOM VEHICLE

The trial of any case in front of a jury is always risky. Most juries are composed of twelve citizens and maybe one or two alternates of different backgrounds, education, and biases. They will listen to the evidence, observe the witnesses, listen to the attorneys' opening statements and closing arguments. Finally, the Court will provide the instructions for the jury to follow and then the jury will go back to the jury room to deliberate. In the Missouri State Circuit Court, only 9 of 12 jurors are needed to reach a verdict. Juries have been known to deliberate for hours, sometimes days and, every once in awhile, less than an hour before reaching a verdict. The time waiting for a jury to return its verdict is the most nerve-racking experience, not just for the client but the attorney who always believes his reputation is on the line.

Most defense attorneys, with their client and the insurance company, can control which cases go to trial. Since the insurance company has the money to pay to plaintiffs – the person who files the suit – the insurance company decides which cases to settle before trial. If the defendant – the person being sued – is truly the cause of plaintiff's damages, then the case should be settled and the amount of damages are determined by the settlement amount. Allowing a jury to set the damages is like giving the jury a blank check. No attorney can control everything that happens in a courtroom during a 3- or 4-day trial. Sometimes something unrelated to the facts of a case could sway a jury's decision.

The following story is an example of the risk of trial by jury even when the facts of the case are totally in the favor of the plaintiff.

My client, George White, had been at a party where approximately twenty-five persons were in attendance. Most of the people had known each other from college or business and had gathered at a friend's house to party at the start of the weekend. The gathering started at about 9:30 p.m. and lasted until the early hours of the next morning. George went to the party with his friend, Dan Groves, whom he had known from high school. Dan and George each drove to the party and met there about 10:00 p.m. One of the guests was a pretty young lady by the name of Nina Russo, who was about 22 years old. Nina had been a ballet dancer since grade school and had become a professional ballerina, appearing in several local productions. Nina, a brunette, was built well, with strong legs you would expect for a dancer. George had known Nina for a few years but had never been involved romantically. They were friends and shared numerous friends from the crowd of persons who generally hung out together. Dan was also friendly with Nina but did not know her as well as George did. Around 12:30 a.m. Nina approached George and asked if he would drive her home. Since Nina lived about 5 miles from George, he agreed to do so. It so happened that Dan was leaving at the same time but was not going as far west as Nina lived, so he could not accommodate Nina to drive her home. All three persons, George, Nina, and Dan had been drinking alcoholic beverages that night. As Nina got into the front passenger seat of George's car, she strapped on her seat belt and waived goodbye to her friends outside. George started his car and proceeded west on Danica Avenue. Dan pulled out just behind George's vehicle and the two cars were about 1–2 car-lengths apart.

Danica was a four-lane street with two lanes for parked cars and one lane eastbound and one lane westbound. George was traveling westbound at about 30 miles per hour, which was the speed limit, when an eastbound vehicle suddenly veered into the westbound lane approximately 100 feet from George's car.

George reacted quickly by turning the steering wheel hard to the right. George's vehicle's right front tire hit the curb and the car jumped the curb and smashed into a large tree about fifteen feet away. Dan, who was traveling about a car-length behind George's vehicle, was able to turn to the right, narrowly missing the eastbound vehicle. The eastbound vehicle continued eastbound and the driver never returned to the accident scene. This car, which didn't stop or return to the scene of this accident, is referred to as a phantom vehicle since no one can identify the make or color of the vehicle, the identity of the driver, or whether any passengers were in the car. The police came to the scene as well as an ambulance to attend to Nina. The police took a statement from my client, George, and the witness, Dan. Nina's statement was given to the police at the hospital.

Nina stated she never saw the unidentified vehicle as she had been looking away and first became aware of anything unusual when the right front tire hit the curb and smashed into the tree. Based on the statements of the only two witnesses, George and Dan, George was not charged with any violation. Fortunately for George, the police were so focused on Nina's injuries they never did a Breathalyzer test on George to see if he had a blood alcohol level that exceeded the legal limit.

Approximately six months after this accident, Nina, at the insistence of her parents, filed a lawsuit against George in excess of $25,000 in damages. George only had minimum limits of $25,000 for liability coverage. Nina had a serious injury to her right ankle, which was fractured in two places, and three right rib fractures. Nina's rib injury had cleared up, but her ankle injury was so severe her dream of dancing professionally as a ballet dancer was no longer possible. Nina's medical bills exceeded $10,000 and the case had a value of $85,000 if George was determined to be the cause of this accident. Nina was totally innocent as to the cause of the accident and no percentage of fault could be placed on her unless drinking at the party became an issue.

The attorney for Nina, Don McManus, agreed not to introduce drinking into evidence in order to prevent me arguing Nina had some fault by getting into a vehicle where the driver had multiple alcoholic drinks at the party, she being aware of that fact. There was a possibility that if drinking was introduced in the trial, a jury would find Nina to be a percentage at fault for voluntarily getting into a vehicle when she knew or should have known the driver was impaired from the alcohol. I readily agreed with Don, Nina's attorney, not to introduce evidence of drinking and the jury would not be aware of this fact.

Prior to the start of trial, Nina's attorney demanded policy limits of $25,000. I countered with an offer of $22,000, stating that my client was not negligent but simply swerved to avoid a head-on collision.

George insisted he did nothing wrong that evening and swerved to avoid hitting the eastbound vehicle that suddenly crossed over the center line into his westbound lane. George was sorry for Nina's injuries, but he did not feel responsible and, in fact, was upset that Nina had sued him.

The trial took place in the City of St. Louis, which was known for being liberal to injured plaintiffs, usually awarding anywhere from seven to ten times as much as the medical bills and lost wages. In this case, this jury, based on past experience, could have returned a verdict against my client for over $100,000. I advised George that he should reconsider and let me offer his policy limits of $25,000, but George was adamant about his position that the accident was not his fault. Besides, George said I have nothing for Nina to take if she gets a judgment for an amount in excess of the $25,000 policy limit. In order to protect myself from a legal malpractice suit, I put George's position on the record that he did not want to offer the policy limits to settle this case.

As a result, the trial started; after one-half day of *voir dire,* where each attorney questions the jury panel, the jury was selected with two additional jurors as alternates.

Plaintiff's attorney called Nina as his first witness. Nina described that she had requested George to drive her home and she had been sitting in the passenger seat with her head back and eyes closed. She could feel the motion of the car and it seemed to be driving at a speed within the 30-mile-per-hour limit and didn't notice anything unusual. Suddenly the car seemed to pull to the right and the tires hit something and almost within an instant came to an abrupt stop.

Her body had been thrown about, but she was held in place by her seatbelt. She remembers pressing her feet against the floorboard and, when the car stopped hard against the tree, her legs were thrown upward under the dash. At first she felt shaken up and sore on her right side. Later her ankle felt swollen and, when she was helped from the car, she had trouble standing, with extreme pain in her ankle.

The next witness called by Plaintiff's attorney was Nina's treating physician, a very qualified orthopedic surgeon. There was no issue about the injuries sustained by Nina, but Nina's attorney wanted to show the damages for future pain and suffering to the jury.

The surgeon was a very athletic-built 55-year-old who explained the extent of Nina's injuries in simple language that any eighth grader would understand. As he explained the seriousness of the multi-fracture of her ankle, the jury appeared to be listening intently. Dr. Rose explained how the healing had not gone as well as he had hoped, but the ankle was stable. He stated that with reasonable medical certainty that Nina would have an arthritic ankle which would cause her much pain. It was Dr. Rose's opinion that Nina would be unable to dance professionally because of this injury which was caused by the collision.

As his last witness, Nina's attorney called Dan. Knowing that Dan would support my client's version of how the accident occurred, Don, Nina's attorney, made the decision that he would rather call Dan Graves as his witness so he could control the questions and topics he wanted the jury to hear before I had called Dan as my witness. I would then be somewhat limited in my cross-examination.

During the direct examination, Dan admitted his close relationship with my client since their high school days. He told the jury he was driving about two car-lengths behind George's vehicle and driving around the speed limit. It was around 1:30 a.m. and they were driving west on a narrow street. The street was dark and no other cars were moving that Dan observed. He could see the rear lights of George's vehicle, but no eastbound cars had passed for at least 5 blocks and probably more.

Dan then described that without warning he observed George's car veer sharply to the right, jump the curb, and smash into a large tree. Dan, of course, had looked toward George's car. As his head was turned toward the right, Dan with peripheral vision saw a vehicle driving east, but only for a split second. Dan admitted to questions from Nina's attorney that he did not know the speed of that eastbound car; he did not know the make or model of that car; he did not know the color; he did not know how many passengers, if any, were in that car; he did not know if the driver was a male or female. Most damaging to my client's theory of his defense, Dan admitted he never saw that eastbound car ever drive in the westbound lane. Nina's attorney did an excellent job of examining the only eyewitness to this accident.

In my cross-exam of Dan, I could only have him tell the jury that although he was a very good friend of George for many years he would never lie under oath for his friend. He also agreed he was a friend of Nina and felt sorry for her injuries and he was there to tell the jury what he saw that night.

I asked Dan if, driving the 10 or 15 minutes he had been following George's car that evening, had he ever seen any evidence of erratic driving by George before that sudden turn to the right. Dan told the jury that George had been driving normal the entire time until just before his car veered to the right and jumped the curb and hit the tree.

Dan ended his testimony by telling the jury he was so concerned with Nina and George his head was turned to the right and his car was facing right to park so he could run to his two friends to assist in any way he could. Dan said as he was looking at George's vehicle he noticed a car passing going eastbound, which took all of about 2–3 seconds. Fortunately Don, the Plaintiff's attorney, as agreed, did not bring out any of the alcohol consumption by any of the three young people.

The attorney for Nina advised the Court that he had no more evidence to introduce and rested his case. The judge then announced a lunch recess and the case would resume at 1:00 p.m. with the start of the Defendant's case.

During the lunch break, I met with George and told him to look squarely at the jury when answering questions. Also, do not hesitate to tell the jury, when describing the eastbound vehicle, which suddenly veered into his lane, how he was forced to take the evasive action he did to avoid a head-on collision. I told him, at some point during his testimony, to let the jury know his concern for Nina's injuries. The one last instruction I gave George was that under no circumstances should he mention that he had any alcoholic beverages that night. I reminded George that Nina's attorney had agreed with my proposal not to bring alcohol consumption into the case.

I had only one witness for the jury in my case. My intent was to get George on and off the stand as quickly as possible. In my experience, the weakest part of most cases is your client's testimony from the witness stand; that is the time for the opposing counsel to discredit your client and raise doubts in the jury's mind about your client's position on the facts. If the opposing attorney is unable to raise doubts about your client's testimony, he should not try the case and should settle or not even file suit in some cases.

When the recess was over and the jury was back in the jury box, we waited patiently for the judge to return to the bench to start my defense. We all waited silently for about 20 minutes before the judge entered the courtroom. Everyone stood out of respect for the position of being judge. As we sat down at the request of the judge, he asked if I was ready to call my first witness. I advised the judge that I was and called my client, George White, to the stand.

As George walked up to take his seat, the bailiff asked him to raise his right hand and swear to tell the truth, which he did.

George made a good appearance but came across a bit nervous, which is not unusual for anyone who has never testified in a courtroom.

I started with the easy background questions so the jury would have some knowledge of who George is. Then I took George through his relationship with Dan and how long they had been close friends. I had George describe his relationship with Nina as being good friends for about four years, but no more involvement than friends. By now George appeared more relaxed and comfortable.

I spent only about two minutes discussing the party and how he agreed to drive Nina home and he was aware Dan was leaving the party at the same time and Dan's route home would follow George's route for most of the trip.

Now I directed George to his car being on Danica driving west on this narrow street. George did well in describing how he only observed Dan's car directly behind his going the speed limit with no vehicles passing him for 4 to 5 blocks going eastbound. George described the music on the radio and, at times, he and Nina had some conversation but very little as she seemed to be resting and listening to the music. George stated at all times he was looking straight ahead and he could see cars parked on both sides of the street.

George then went on to state he saw headlights coming east, which appeared to be coming up a hill. Then George described how this eastbound vehicle suddenly came over into the middle of the westbound lane. George guessed that the distance between his vehicle and the eastbound vehicle was about 150 feet.

George said his first reaction was to swerve to the right as hard as he could. He then described a jolt when his right front wheel hit the curb and the car went onto a grassy area about 25 feet, stopping by crashing hard into a large tree.

George said he tried to apply the brakes after turning the steering wheel as far right as possible and didn't know if the speed reduced much from the 25 miles per hour he had been traveling when the collision occurred.

George went on to state he first went to help Nina as she was in obvious pain. He described how the police arrived and an ambulance at about the same time. He was not aware who had called them. George went on to describe how the medical persons attended to Nina and she left the scene in the ambulance. Then, without being asked a question, George, looking at Nina, said: "I am truly sorry, Nina, for your injury. I took the only action I could to avoid a head-on collision."

Nina's attorney, Don, jumped up immediately with a proper objection, stating this voluntary statement of George was not responsive to any question and asked the judge to instruct the jury to disregard George's statement. This was a very good objection and the judge did as Don requested.

The problem is that the jury heard the comment and asking them to disregard this statement is like having the whipped cream on top of the sundae put back in the can. It can't be done. I had no more questions for George and told the Court I had completed my direct examination.

The judge told the jury that they have now heard all of the evidence and we will adjourn for the day as he and the lawyers will meet the rest of the afternoon to work on the final instructions that will be read to the jury before closing arguments.

Don and I met with the judge after the jury was discharged in the judge's chambers.

The judge had a small round table where we were all seated. The judge had removed his long black robe and rolled up his sleeves and loosened his tie. Both Don and I had removed our jackets and sat patiently waiting for the judge to ask us each for the instructions we had prepared for him to read to the jury.

The judge turned to me and asked if I wanted to settle the case, as he believed the jury was going to award Nina a substantial sum of money based on the evidence presented. The judge went on to point out that Nina had done nothing to cause this accident and there would be no fault assessed to her.

I told Judge Adolph that my client insists he took evasive action and was simply not at fault. I went on to state that if Don, Nina's attorney, wanted to make a demand less than the policy limits, I would discuss it with my client.

Judge Adolph turned to Don and asked if he would consider anything less than policy limits to settle this case. Don responded that he was convinced the jury was going to award damages in a sum greater than $100,000 and he was not willing to discuss anything less than the policy limits.

With settlement discussions completed, we went to working on the instructions that the Court would read to the jury before closing arguments. The judge said that we would begin reading the jury instructions at 9 a.m. to be followed by closing arguments.

As I left the courthouse, a light snow was falling and the temperature had dropped to about 28 degrees. The forecast was for the temperature to drop to a high of 18 degrees the next morning with intermittent snow all day.

As I walked from the parking lot four blocks away to the courthouse the next morning, the wind was blowing at the corner of 11th Street and Market as it usually does all year long. Lawyers with briefcases were climbing the steps to the front door. The usual group of sheriff's deputies were hanging out in the lobby outside the sheriff's office, and numerous persons were coming in and out of the ten elevators located on both sides of the building.

I took the elevator to the 7th floor and George was seated on the hard wooden bench outside of Division 9, where our case was being tried. George was fairly calm for a person who was about to be judged by a jury of his peers. The jury consisted of 7 people over 45 years of age and 5 less than 45. There were 4 women and 8 men on the jury.

The attorney for Nina was already seated at the counsel table appearing to be writing notes, which I suppose was for his closing argument. Don McManus told the judge he wanted 20 minutes for his closing argument and 5 minutes for rebuttal. Since I had no right to rebuttal, I told the judge I wanted the full 25 minutes but would try to complete my closing in less time.

The bailiff came out to the courtroom and told Don and me he was going to bring the jury out as the judge was ready to start. The bailiff went back to get the jury and I told George to sit and face the jury during closing argument and make no facial reaction to any comments about him by Nina's attorney. I told George that the jury will be watching him during the closing argument.

The jury then walked into the courtroom and went to the same seats they had occupied for the last four days. Most of the jurors had sweaters and two had their coats on. Shortly the judge entered, and as he did, everyone rose and Judge Adolph advised them to be seated.

The judge seemed to be straightening the space in front of him and picked up the 11 instructions and bounced them against his desk in a neat package and put a paperclip on them. Then, in what seemed to be an unusual move, the judge motioned the attorneys to approach the bench.

Don McManus, Nina's attorney, was a slender-built man about 5-foot-9 and weighed some 160 pounds. McManus, a man with bright red hair, stood up first and I followed a few steps behind. When we both reached the side bar with our backs to the jury, the judge said very softly: "Please raise the window slightly as the courtroom is too warm." Knowing that it was freezing outside with a blowing wind, I went back to my seat with no intention of following the judge's request unless he asked me loud enough for the jury to hear. Don also sat down but, seeing that I wasn't moving toward the window, got up and walked over to the window and stood with his back to the jury. With both arms spread and each hand on a metal handle at the bottom of the window, he tugged at the window which, after several tugs, raised about six inches.

As I sat staring straight ahead, I felt a cold breeze come across my body from the area where the window was raised. I heard some grumbling from my left and, as I turned, noticed several jurors appearing to be hugging themselves with frowns on their faces.

Then the judge turned to Don and said: "Counsel, would you please lower that window some." There was no doubt in my mind that every juror felt that Don, on his own, made the decision to open the window and let the cold air blow through the room. Hopefully no juror had noticed the smile that came across my face.

Don started his closing argument by thanking the jury for spending their time to decide this case. The fact of the matter is they had no choice. They had been summoned by law to appear as potential jurors; failure to do so could cause them to be jailed, fined a sum of money, or both. Don was smart enough to spend most of the opening portion of his closing argument telling the jury about Nina's serious injuries, especially her fractured ankle. He went on to state what a very good career she was hoping to have as a ballet dancer and now that dream is gone, all as a result of the negligence of my client.

Don then explained to the jury that the defense of a phantom vehicle suddenly veering into George's westbound lane is not credible. The only person to support George's version as to how the collision occurred was his best friend, Dan, whom George knew since grade school. Naturally Don went on to argue that these long-term friends for over 20-plus years would have the same story.

Don argued further to the jury that neither George nor Dan could tell the jury the make or model of the car or the color of the car. They couldn't tell the jury whether the driver of that eastbound car was male or female. Further the two men couldn't say whether there were any passengers in that car. The reason, Don said, is that there *was* no eastbound car. George, Don went on to argue, just lost control of the car, hit the curb, and smashed into the tree, causing the serious injuries Nina had. Don closed by asking the jury to award Nina $250,000 for her past and future medical bills, the pain and suffering Nina sustained, and the lost chance to become a very good professional ballerina.

I thought Don had done an excellent job in the opening portion of his closing argument and I could see the jury looking in Nina's direction and feeling Nina's loss. I felt certain they wanted to give her some monetary award.

As I rose to begin my closing argument, I knew I had to acknowledge Nina's injuries and not diminish them.

I started out by telling the jury how sorry my client and I are for the injuries Nina sustained. I have much sympathy for her and the fact she may never dance professionally as a ballerina.

I went on to state that the instructions given by the Court specifically say not to consider sympathy for either party during your deliberations.

The Court instructs you to be guided by the evidence presented to you by both sides. The instructions also tell you that before you can consider a monetary award for Nina, you must first find my client was negligent.

In this case, you heard George and Dan talk about an eastbound vehicle that suddenly swerved into George's westbound lane so close to George that he quickly took evasive action – swerving to the right, causing his tire to jump the curb, smashing into a tree. That, I told the jury, would not be negligence.

I went on to state that Nina's attorney argued there was no eastbound car, no phantom car, as testified to by both my client and his best friend. I told the jury this entire case narrowed down to one issue, the phantom eastbound car.

If the jury found that there was an eastbound car that suddenly veered into George's westbound lane, they must return a verdict in favor of my client, no matter how much sympathy they had for Nina because of her injuries.

I then went on to state that Nina's attorney was absolutely correct when he told you neither George nor Dan could tell you the make or model, the color, whether the driver was male or female, or how many people were in that phantom car. I then paused and walked slowly behind Nina sitting next to her attorney. I let the silence linger for about 45 seconds, which seemed like 2 minutes. The jurors were looking at me, waiting.

I then, in a loud voice, said we could have been able to identify the make and model of that eastbound car as well as its color and the identity of the driver. We could have also told you how many passengers were in that eastbound car. I hesitated for about 15 seconds and then, in a much lower voice, went on and said: "To do so, my client George would have had to fail to take evasive action and hit the eastbound car head-on, bringing it to a stop so that all of the questions asked by Nina's attorney could be answered." I then pointed to Nina and said, but this young lady may not have been here. Instead, her estate would be bringing this case. George, I went on to say, saved Nina's life by taking this evasive action and you should find in favor of my client.

I paused briefly and then I stood behind my client and placed both hands on George's shoulders. I said to the jury: "My client has lived with this burden of being blamed for all of Nina's injuries and you, the jury, now have the key to lifting this heavy weight from my client. I believe, as you will deliberate all the facts you have heard during this trial, you will make the right decision." I thanked the jury and, as I passed by my client, dropped my hand on his shoulder for a brief moment and took my seat.

Don, Nina's attorney, spent his 5 minutes of rebuttal once again outlining the injuries sustained by his client and her lost dream of dancing professionally.

The judge then asked the bailiff to take the jury instructions and escort the jury to the jury room. All the jurors left the courtroom except the two alternates. Although they sat through the entire trial, the alternates are not allowed to deliberate the verdict. The judge advised the alternates that they are now free to talk with the attorneys about the case if they wish, but they do not have to.

It was never something I would do because, in my experience, I found when talking to an alternate that individual would usually tell the attorney what he thought the attorney wanted to hear. The alternate did not have the benefit of listening to the other jurors and listening to how they viewed the evidence. I always felt a jury, after deliberating for several hours or more, takes on the personality of those more forceful and persuasive jurors on any jury. I refer to these jurors as "chiefs." It is fortunate if you have two or three chiefs on your jury. The remaining jurors I refer to as "Indians" as the majority of jurors will follow the lead of the chiefs. A good trial attorney will identify the chiefs on the jury panel during the *voir dire* examination. If you identify the chiefs on *voir dire* and you believe they are likely to support your position, you try to keep them on the final jury selection. On the other hand, if you believe that a chief would not support your position, you wisely use one of your three strikes to remove that particular juror from the final jury.

The jury left the courtroom at 1:45 p.m. The lawyers, like myself, are returning phone calls to persons they couldn't talk to during the trial. The litigants like Nina and George are nervously waiting for the jury to reach its verdict. Time seems to stand still as each minute seems like ten.

The one thing for me as a trial attorney that is most difficult and I believe is the reason very few lawyers are trial attorneys is the immediate result that a jury delivers.

A trial attorney can spend almost two years and sometimes longer from the first meeting with a client to trial. During that time, the attorney has labored through hearings in Court on various motions, taking numerous depositions of witnesses, parties, and sometimes experts. The trial attorney then will spend numerous hours preparing for trial. Finally, the trial starts and the trial attorney will have sleepless nights as he prepares for each day of testimony and worries as to how the jury is reacting to the evidence presented. The trial attorney also has to contend with the judge and the unfavorable ruling which comes during any trial. Then after going through many months of concern and self-doubt, the case finally goes to the jury, who could deliberate for hours or days but that jury will return its verdict at some point. The waiting for the verdict is difficult for the most seasoned attorney.

These factors are the reasons most attorneys do not want to be trial attorneys.

It has been almost two hours since the jury retired to deliberate and the buzzer rang once. This meant there was a question from the jury.

The attorneys went into the judge's chambers and the question was written on a yellow notepad and signed by the foreperson. The judge identified the foreperson as the woman in the second row, 6th seat in the jury box. This juror was a chief. The question could have been from one or more of the jurors and it was simple. The question asked if Nina had any insurance to cover her medical expenses.

Insurance by law is not allowed to be discussed or presented in evidence in most trials by jury unless the insurance carrier is a party to the suit or the policy is put into evidence.

Lawyers always speculate as to what a question from a jury means as to how the jury is thinking. In this case, I could interpret this either way as being favorable to both Nina and George.

As I expected, Judge Adolph wrote a response saying that he cannot respond to that question and the jury is to be guided only by the evidence they have heard in this case. Both attorneys on the record agreed with this response. The judge handed his response to the bailiff who went back to the jury room to deliver the judge's response. The bailiff always sits outside the jury room to make sure no one enters or leaves without permission.

It took the jury about another 75 minutes before they reached a verdict. The buzzer rang twice and the bailiff went to tell the judge. Then the bailiff went out in the hallway where the parties and attorneys were and told them the verdict had been reached.

The judge came from his chambers to the courtroom and waited until the attorneys and parties were seated. The judge then requested the bailiff to bring the jury in. It took about 10 minutes before the jury of twelve came back to the jury box, each carrying the coats, sweaters, and scarves. They knew they were going home after the verdict is read and not back to that small jury room.

When everyone was seated, the judge said on the record: "Has the jury reached its verdict?"

The foreperson stood up with the verdict form and instructions in her hand. "Yes, we have," she replied.

The judge instructed her to give the papers to the bailiff, which she did. The bailiff removed the verdict form from all of the papers and handed it to the judge. The judge looked at the verdict form, reading the results, and then handed the verdict form to the bailiff and instructed him to read the verdict. This process took all of two minutes, but it seemed like an eternity. No matter how many jury verdicts I have heard read by a bailiff, it never gets easier. My stomach is churning, my throat is dry, and I am certain my heart rate jumps 40 points.

Now the verdict is read: "We, the jury, find in favor of the Defendant, George White." Signed by the foreperson only, which means a unanimous verdict.

I hear an immediate scream from across the room. "Oh, no!" Nina cried out. I then heard her sobbing.

George, of course, was elated and jumped up, grabbing me and thanking me. I felt very good, of course, winning for my client. I could not help feeling sorry for Nina, who had rejected our offer and will end up with no money.

I personally did not know whether there ever was a phantom car as George and Dan had testified. I only presented the evidence in a light most favorable to my client.

I have often wondered whether the fact that Nina's attorney had raised the window on that cold morning just before starting his closing argument played any part in this verdict that was unfavorable to him and his client.

This is something I will never know, but I will always wonder.

CHAPTER VII

⋖⋗⋘⋙⋖⋗

KISS IN THE NIGHT

About 10:30 a.m. my partner, Jerry Kraus, came into my office to discuss a case he had decided to take. The client had sustained a serious injury: a fractured left knee and ankle. The suit would have to be filed against our client's insurance company since the driver of the other vehicle was driving without insurance. As Jerry described, there was only one problem which was liability. The facts were that our client had been in a neighborhood bar drinking from 5 p.m. until 10 p.m. Our client, John Elliot, left the bar and eventually drove west on a two-lane road and traveled on the eastbound side of the road and came into contact with an eastbound vehicle and went off the road and struck a telephone pole with the front of his car. His major injury was the fractured left knee and ankle. John had other injuries, mostly cuts and bruises and lots of pain. The client's blood alcohol level was 2.6, more than twice the legal limit at that time which was 1.0. Further, the client had pled guilty to driving while intoxicated and lost his license for one year. Jerry then said that the case was set for trial in four months and he was unable to obtain an offer to settle. The case was also difficult since the other uninsured driver had not been found and our client had no recollection of the facts since he was so intoxicated. To make matters worse, the defense attorney, Paul Brown, was one of the best in the business.

The only way I could ever win this case was under the "Last Clear Chance Doctrine." This trial was before Missouri adopted Comparative Fault. Contributory Negligence before Comparative Fault was a complete bar to any recovery by the plaintiff. Since my client was negligent, there was no way I could win this case unless I could prove my client was in a position of peril and the uninsured motorist had the last clear chance with safety to himself and others to avoid the collision. At the time I agreed to try the case, I had no such evidence to support a last clear chance theory.

About two months before the trial, I received a notice of deposition from Paul Brown's office. They had found the driver of the uninsured car and had set his deposition in a small town about 50 miles south of St. Louis.

Since I was unavailable for the date the deposition was set, my partner, Don Sherman, agreed to attend the deposition. This would be our one and only opportunity to make a case under the Last Clear Chance Doctrine. This opportunity was handed to us by the defense attorney. There would be no reason for the defense to set this deposition unless they felt this case was one they could not lose under any circumstances, and this was confirmed when I tried to settle this case just prior to the start of trial.

Don did an excellent job, as usual, with the examination of the uninsured motorist. The key portion of his deposition was that he had seen my client's car proceeding west and was halfway over the center line in the eastbound lane. At that point, my client's vehicle was about 750 to 1,000 feet from the vehicle of the uninsured motorist. The driver went on to state that within 3–5 seconds the two cars passed and just barely clipped each other and my client's vehicle swerved to the left off the highway and into a post. The uninsured driver stopped and went back to my client's vehicle and waited until the police came. He waited until the ambulance took my client from the scene and then left. The driver admitted that he had no insurance at the time of the accident because he had missed several monthly payments and was cancelled a few months before this accident.

I now had enough facts to get to a jury under the Last Clear Chance Doctrine, but this was still a bad case to try even though the defendant was my client's insurance company. The facts remained that my client was drunk and driving his vehicle on the wrong side of the road. Fortunately for everyone, my client was the only one injured.

On the day of trial, I appeared with my client. Paul Brown and I both announced ready for trial and we were assigned to a civil division. The judge asked if we could settle the case and I was willing to recommend

$2,500 to settle since, in my mind, I had little chance to get a favorable verdict. Paul Brown said he had no authority from his client to make any offer and the case would have to be tried.

Paul went on to make one of the most unforgettable statements I have heard in my career, which was, "If I lose this case, then I will surrender my license." In essence, Paul was declaring this case was an absolute winner. There is NO such case when decided by a jury.

The evidence came in as expected. The jury was told about my client's heavy drinking and the fact he was driving on the wrong side of the road when the collision occurred. Two unexpected events happened during the two-day trial. First was the testimony regarding the blood alcohol level. Rather than letting the officer testify as to the results of the test showing the level at 2.6, I asked to *voir dire* the officer out of the hearing of the jury.

The *voir dire* revealed that the officer, after taking my client's blood, simply took the sample home and put it in his refrigerator, which was against protocol. In addition, the sample the officer took was passed to the final testing person but had been in the hands of an unknown individual and that was not recorded. As a result, the chain of control was broken and unaccounted for. I requested the Court disallow the test showing the blood alcohol level of my client and the judge agreed. As a result, the jury never heard of my client's blood alcohol level. The only testimony regarding my client's drinking that night was my client's testimony that in the five hours my client was at the bar he had approximately 10 beers, which did not sound as bad as 2.6 blood alcohol level.

The second event that helped my case was the testimony of the uninsured motorist. As he did in his deposition, he described my client driving on the wrong side of the road about 1,000 feet from his vehicle as he observed my client's headlights. He was unable to say whether my client was exceeding the 40-mile-per-hour speed limit and other than being on the wrong side of the road the witness could not testify as to any other erratic driving.

The other driver went on to state that he fully expected my client to get back over to his westbound lane but, as the distance between the two cars closed to within 200 feet, the uninsured driver moved several feet to the right to avoid the oncoming collision but was not successful. He went on to testify that the cars slightly touched as they passed and he saw my client's vehicle go to the left and into a telephone pole.

I asked the witness if he felt as if the two cars slightly touched as if a slight "kiss in the night" as they passed. Fortunately, the witness agreed.

Seeing an opportunity of supporting my theory of putting my client in a position of peril and the uninsured driver having the last clear chance of avoiding the accident, I went into questioning as to positioning of his vehicle just prior to the two vehicles coming into contact.

The uninsured motorist told the jury that about 200 feet from contact he realized unless he took action there would be an accident. He said he swerved two or three feet to the right in the second or two before the accident and the cars just touched as they passed like a "kiss in the night."

I asked the driver what distance separated the right side of his car to the end of the traveled portion of the highway and he responded approximately two feet. I went on to inquire if there was a shoulder adjacent to the highway and, if so, what was the width of the shoulder.

Fortunately, the witness said the shoulder was approximately five feet wide. This meant that the uninsured driver had another seven feet to swerve.

My next question to this key witness was the following: "You would agree that if you moved another four feet to the right, which would have put you two feet on the right shoulder, you would not have made contact with my client's vehicle and the kiss would never have occurred." The witness agreed. My last question was that he could have avoided contact with my client's vehicle in sufficient time and with safety to himself and others to which he also agreed. As a result, I had put my client in a position of peril and the uninsured motorist had the last clear chance to avoid the accident.

In my closing argument to the jury, I admitted that my client, John Elliott, obviously had too much to drink and was obviously negligent in driving on the wrong side of the road, but under the current law the jury had to find in his favor.

There was no question that the other driver was driving without insurance and therefore my client was entitled to the compensation under the Uninsured Motorist provision of his auto policy. There was no question that John had been seriously injured with a knee and ankle fractures. I went on to tell the jury the only issue was whether the uninsured driver had the Last Clear Chance to avoid the accident when my client had obviously placed himself in a position of peril.

I argued that all the testimony from the uninsured driver supported the conclusion that had he swerved just 2–3 feet they would have avoided the accident and as a result, in spite of John Elliott's negligence, he should receive a favorable verdict for the limits of the policy.

As in every case I try, the last words I convey to the jury are that I have had the responsibility of representing my client for over the last 18 months and I have carried this burden for this length of time or however long I have had the case. I go on to state that I am now lifting this burden from my shoulders and placing it squarely on the shoulders of this jury. I then end by saying my client and I will be here waiting for your verdict. I thank them and sit down. The jury then is escorted from the courtroom to the jury room to deliberate. In this case, I was not exactly truthful. As soon as the jury left the courtroom, I told my client I had a meeting and would return as soon as I could but that the clerk would call me if there was a verdict. When I left the courthouse, I felt I had a chance to win but the negligence of my client was so bad I felt there was a strong possibility that I would lose this case.

I went to my meeting and returned almost two hours later. I took the elevator to the 6th floor where the courtroom was located. As soon as I stepped off the elevator, I saw my jury in the hall outside the courtroom. When I asked what they were doing, one of the jurors said they had reached a verdict in favor of my client, John Elliott, for the full amount of the uninsured motorist coverage in the policy.

I saw Paul Brown in the courtroom and I told him that he did not have to surrender his license, as he initially stated if he lost this case.

The point is that there is a risk to any case that is decided by a jury. No attorney, no matter how good the facts or the ability of the attorney, can guaranty a winner.

CHAPTER VIII

LAST CLEAR CHANCE

I received a call one morning from Dave Sands asking if I could help him out with a case he had pending in Baltimore, Maryland. He had retained an experienced defense lawyer to defend this case, but was not happy with the way this attorney was reporting about the status of the case and potential damages which could be incurred if an unfavorable verdict.

Dave said that a young salesman employed by the dealer had been out the evening of the accident and had a few drinks but his blood alcohol level was just below the legal limit. The driver had been charged with driving under the influence (DUI) as opposed to driving while intoxicated (DWI).

Dave provided me with the following details of events. The salesman, Alex Turner, was alone at about 12:30 a.m. driving a brand new Buick LaSabre down the highway when his headlights picked up a middle-aged man staggering in the middle of the highway. The man appeared to be about 50 yards in front of Alex, who was moving at 80 miles per hour, which equals 120 feet per second. This gave Alex no time to avoid hitting this individual since, with the additional time it took Alex to react to this dangerous situation, Alex could not avoid striking this unfortunate drunk. The pedestrian was knocked flying through the air and ended up over 100 feet from the point of impact. Alex brought his vehicle to a stop 60 yards past the point he struck the pedestrian.

Visibly shaken, Alex called the police and explained the situation. Within 10 minutes the police and an ambulance arrived at the scene.

The drunk, who was identified as William Hanks, was given first aid at the scene and taken by ambulance to the nearest hospital.

The medical records revealed that William suffered multiple fractures in all limbs, as well as cuts and bruises. Luckily there were no head injuries.

According to Dave, William's four-day hospital stay cost $118,000. His doctor's bill was over $40,000. William had a part-time job without health insurance to pay his medical bills. With loss of wages and physical therapy, William Hanks had specials totaling close to $200,000. The demand to settle this case was $750,000, and Dave wanted me to work with the local counsel in the defense of this case. Dave said that the local counsel, Martin Dicker, was aware that I was going to join him in the defense of this case and I was to be lead counsel.

I flew to Baltimore the next week and took a room in a nice hotel in the Harbour area. Martin picked me up at the scheduled time in an eight-year-old Chevrolet. As I entered the car, I saw a man of about 62 years of age smoking a cigarette. The ashtray was open and filled with ashes and butts. The car wreaked of smoke and the windows had a tint of smoke which could not be removed with a wet cloth. Martin drove to a neighborhood restaurant that specialized in fresh crab. The tablecloths were red checkered and every one of the wait staff and bartender welcomed Martin as we walked to our table. Evidently Martin was a regular.

The first ½ hour I learned that Martin had been an attorney for 34 years and spent most of his time defending automobile cases for insurance companies. He most recently left a three-man partnership to work on his own with one secretary and a part-time lawyer. Martin was apparently burnt out as a trial attorney and was staying in the practice because he had nothing else that would provide him with an income.

I had the impression that at one time Martin had been an excellent attorney. I later found out that some personal problems led to excessive drinking, which caused his removal from his previous partnership. He was able to hold onto enough insurance defense business to survive in the practice of law, which admittedly, Martin did not like any longer.

As we talked about the case, Martin said there was one guy who had been with William Hanks all evening but had not been identified in the police report. This person was identified in the answer to interrogations provided by Hanks. The address for the witness was no longer valid and

Martin had been unsuccessful in finding him. The witness was Angelo Carton. Martin went on to state that the deposition of the plaintiff needed to be taken and the Court had ordered mediation to be completed within the next 90 days.

Both Martin and I agreed that the injuries were severe and, just based on injuries alone, the verdict could be as low as $500,000 and as high as $1,000.000.

Almost every state had adopted the "Comparative Fault" doctrine, which meant even if the plaintiff was a percentage of fault any verdict would be reduced by the percentage of fault attributed to the plaintiff. Thus, if a million-dollar verdict was awarded to the plaintiff and he was assessed 50 percent of fault, the net award to the plaintiff was $500,000.

Maryland was different. At the time of this case, Maryland still had not adopted the Comparative Fault Doctrine. Maryland still worked under Contributory Negligence. This meant if the plaintiff was assessed any part of fault in this case, the plaintiff was barred from any recovery. Thus in this case, if Plaintiff William Hanks was 10 percent at fault and my client was 90 percent at fault, the plaintiff would receive nothing for his injuries.

There was one exception to Contributory Negligence: this was the Last Clear Chance Doctrine. Under this doctrine, if the plaintiff was in a "position of peril" and the defendant had the last chance to avoid the accident, then in that event the plaintiff was not barred by his own negligence to recover a verdict for damages. What was a "position of peril" as well as "last clear chance" was for the jury to decide.

Based on the facts as I knew them at the time I arrived in Baltimore, this was a case that a good plaintiff's attorney could present to the jury as the exception to the contributory negligence doctrine. A good plaintiff's attorney could argue that the plaintiff was obviously negligent by being intoxicated and placing himself in a position of peril by walking out in the traveled portion of the highway. The attorney could then argue that my client had the last clear chance to avoid the collision with the plaintiff if he kept a lookout. The car my client was driving had headlights that would have shined on the plaintiff 100 yards away and, if my client was attentive, he had plenty of time to swerve two lanes to the right and avoid the collision. This was certainly a case that could be won by a good plaintiff's attorney, and a verdict in excess of one-half million dollars was certainly possible.

The attorney representing Hanks was not a seasoned trial attorney. The attorney, Bill Londo, had been practicing for over 10 years. He had a reputation of being a person who would rather settle a case than try the case.

I met the plaintiff Hanks for the first time when I took his deposition. Hanks was about 42 years old and was dressed in a short-sleeved shirt and slacks, both of which showed signs of wear and tear. His hair was starting to thin and he never looked me in the eye when responding to questions.

Hanks admitted to having at least three cocktails and a number of beers, but could not state how many. The most damaging testimony to his case came when he denied being in the middle of the road when he was struck by my client's vehicle. Hanks insisted that he was on the side of the road and Alex drove his car off the road and struck Hanks and swerved back on the road, coming to a stop in the middle of the road many feet past where Hanks was hit. Hanks could not state how many feet Alex's vehicle had traveled after it came into contact with him.

The testimony provided by Hanks was not supported by the physical facts at the scene. The investigation showed that the broken glass from the vehicle that struck Hanks was in the middle of the road as well as the skid marks from the vehicle that were made after the collision between Hanks and the vehicle. There was no physical evidence to support Hanks' testimony that he was struck while standing on the side of the road.

Hanks' deposition testimony made it impossible to argue the Last Clear Chance Doctrine and as a result Hanks would lose the case based on his contributory negligence for being intoxicated and being in the roadway. There were no witnesses who could place Hanks in a position of peril where my client would have had the last clear chance to avoid the collision. The only possible witness to the collision, Angelo Carton, was nowhere to be found; since the plaintiff could not provide any contact information, the Court agreed to sustain our motion to strike Carton as a witness until such time as he could be produced for deposition. The Court argued that it would not be fair to the defense if suddenly Carton would appear as a witness at trial.

Both Martin Dicker and I appeared at the mediation with our client. The plaintiff's attorney, Bill Londo, presented his opening statement and simply told the mediator that my client left the highway and struck Hanks, who was standing on the side of the road and, as a result, his client sustained serious and permanent injuries. Londo said he wanted $750,000 to settle this case but was willing to negotiate.

I took the position that even though Hanks had suffered serious injuries, he was barred from any recovery because of his contributory negligence. Further, my client was willing to offer some money, but it would not be anywhere near plaintiff's demand of $750,000.

The mediator then met with each side separately in what is referred to as caucus. During the caucus with myself and local counsel, Martin Dicker, I explained to the mediator that I felt we could successfully defend this case because of the position the plaintiff's attorney was taking. I explained that the only possible way the plaintiff could have a chance to win this case had been abandoned by the plaintiff and, in my opinion, the only value this case has to the plaintiff is the cost of defense, which was no more than $35,000. The mediator off the record agreed with my position based on the facts presented.

The mediator then left our room and went to meet in caucus with Plaintiff Hanks and his attorney, Bill Londo. After about forty minutes passed, the mediator knocked on our door and, when he entered the room, he had a slight smile. He said that the plaintiff's attorney has just now become aware of the huge burden he had to meet even to get a jury to decide the case. Although there was no question of the plaintiff's serious injuries, the question of contributory negligence on the plaintiff was so great there was little chance of winning the case. As a result, the plaintiff's attorney has dropped his demand to $150,000.

I called the adjuster, Dave Sands, and told him that the plaintiff had dropped his demand from $750,000 to $150,000. I went on to tell Dave that if the case is tried I expect to get a verdict in favor of my client. I estimated the amount of attorney fees and costs would be between $40,000 and $60,000. Dave gave me authority up to $60,000 to settle the case.

I asked the mediator to advise Bill Londo that I could offer $25,000 to settle this case, but rather than negotiate further I would add another $5000 for a total settlement of $30,000. I suggested that my client's insurance carrier may withdraw the offer if not accepted and proceed to trial. I felt that the threat of withdrawing the offer would put added pressure on the plaintiff's attorney as he realized he would probably lose the case.

The mediator then went to meet with Londo and his client and spent no more than 10 minutes with them. When the mediator returned, he said that Londo and his client would accept the offer of $30,000 but asked and not demanded if we would pay all costs including the mediation. This additional request was less than another $5,000 and of course I agreed to this and the case was settled.

The above story was about a case in which the lawyer was not familiar with nor did he understand the Last Clear Chance Doctrine.

EPILOGUE

In writing this book, it allowed me to introduce the reader to the exciting world of a civil trial attorney.

Sanford Goffstein

ABOUT THE AUTHOR

Sanford Goffstein has been a trial attorney for over fifty years. Most of his legal career has been defending professionals such as lawyers, doctors, accountants, insurance brokers, automobile dealers, among others. He has tried cases throughout the United States.

He graduated law school from Washington University in St. Louis in 1960 and immediately started his own law firm. In October 1961, just a little more than a year after starting his law firm, he was activated into the air force as his Air National Guard unit was called to active duty as a result of the Berlin Wall being constructed. He had to close his law firm while on active duty and started again after serving one year in the service.

Sanford has served as an adjunct professor at Washington University, teaching trial practice and providing students his knowledge and personal experience in the trial of civil cases. This is the first book written by the author. He has chosen stories that may bear some resemblance to actual cases he has handled, but for the most part, the names of the people are fictitious.

The author has attempted to show with these stories how interesting and enjoyable the life of a trial attorney can be. The author is continuing to try civil cases at eighty years of age and still enjoys the action in the courtroom.

www.ingramcontent.com/pod-product-compliance
Lightning Source LLC
Chambersburg PA
CBHW021956170526
45157CB00003B/1021